ISLAM

an illustrated history

THIS IS A CARLTON BOOK

Text copyright © 2002 Michael Jordan
Design copyright © 2002 Carlton Books Limited

This edition published by Carlton Books Limited 2002
20 Mortimer Street
London
W1T 3JW

A CIP catalogue record for this book is available
from the British Library.

ISBN 1 84222 609 6

Printed in Dubai

ISLAM

an illustrated history

Michael Jordan

CARLTON
BOOKS

CONTENTS

WHAT IS ISLAM?

IN OUR TWENTY-FIRST-CENTURY WORLD, THREE GLOBAL RELIGIONS COMPETE with one another in their recognition of one all-powerful and all-seeing God who surpasses any others in his excellence. The proper term for this belief in a pre-eminent, transcendent deity is monotheism and of the three monotheistic faiths, Judaism is the oldest having been established about three and a half thousand years ago while Christianity has just passed the two-millennium mark. Islam is the youngest of these global faiths.

The trio does not represent all the religions in the history of humankind that have worshipped a single omnipotent God. Arguably Zoroastrianism, the ancient religion of Persia against which the Prophet Muhammad pitted himself, should be included since it recognized one divine spark, Ahura Mazda. So too, if one travels even further back in time, should that of the Egyptian ruler Akhenaten, who lived in the second millennium BCE and who believed that the pantheon of Egyptian deities must be swept aside and replaced by one supreme

creator deity. Yet these and others did not stand the test of time, although in fairness remnants of Zoroastriansim do still survive in parts of the world today. There is also a good argument that Hinduism, with all its vast family of gods and goddesses who oversee practically every aspect of life and death, boils down to a kind of monotheism. Each member of the Hindu pantheon can be seen an aspect or variety of the three great creator gods – Brahma, Vishnu and Shiva – and each of these is but a facet of the one unchangeable force of existence. Hinduism, though, does not openly proclaim monotheism in the style of Judaism, Christianity and Islam.

One might also perhaps ask why Buddhism is not included in the list since Buddhists look to a single icon in their belief. Buddhism, however, is quite different in its doctrine, in that the Buddha is not seen as a transcendent god, different in substance from mortal humanity. The Buddha was a living person who achieved a state of perfection and so entered *nirvana* or Paradise, breaking as he did so the wheel of *samsara*, the otherwise endless cycle of life and death. His state of perfection is one for which Buddhists strive but they do not worship him as God.

Perhaps the first potential for misunderstanding that needs clearing up about Islam is in the identity of the God to whom Muslims bow. Each of the three monotheistic religions is not merely dedicated to the worship of a transcendent deity, but each recognizes the *same* God, albeit one who is known by different names. He is Yahweh or El in the Jewish tradition, the medieval Christians knew him as Jehovah and to Muslims he is Allah.

Yet in spite of this mutual bond of belief, while most people in the West are familiar with at least some of the history, belief and traditions of Judaism and Christianity, the same cannot generally be said about Islam.

Previous page: A ceramic tile with abstract plant patterns decorating the mimbar or pulpit from which a khateeb delivers his sermon. The words read, "There is no God but God; Muhammad is His prophet; may God show mercy on Him".

Above: Words from the Holy Qur'an provide the source for an inscription on this tilework in the mosque at Gocek, Turkey.

Opposite: Traditions shared with Judaism are revealed in this manuscript by Loqman, dating from 1583, in which the story of Jonah and the whale are depicted with the Old Testament prophet Jeremiah looking on.

Not least among the reasons for the shortfall in our knowledge is where and how the respective traditions of the three religions are preserved. Many of those belonging to Judaism and Christianity, the narratives that amount to the history, regulations and prophecies of the faith, appear in the same familiar source of information, the books that make up the Old Testament. These form the first half of the Holy Bible, a copy of which most of us possess somewhere in our homes and its popular stories are familiar to us because we learned them at Sunday school, in the classroom and, if we attended church, from the lectern. Islam actually shares many of these traditions, recognizing a surprising number of events and personalities found in the Old Testament, particularly those recorded in the first five books of the Bible known as the Pentateuch. It accepts the validity and the underlying morality contained in accounts such as those of the Garden of Eden, the Flood and Noah's Ark, the destruction of Sodom and Gomorrah, and the escape of the Israelite tribes from Egypt under the leadership of Moses. It also recognizes such Christian figures as Jesus and Mary. Muhammad, the founder of Islam, seems to have venerated many of the Jewish patriarchs and later biblical personalities, believing that they were prophets, forerunners of himself, who had lived in bygone times but who proclaimed the same vision of obedience to the laws of God. Such was Muhammad's benevolence towards Christians that he referred to them warmly as "the people of the book", and had some of the Jews who were his contemporaries not tended to oppose him he might have extended the hand of friendship equally in their direction.

Muslims do not, however, use the Old Testament as a source of scripture and their versions of events seem to come from a different literary origin than the

Bible, perhaps from the Talmud, the code of Jewish civil and canonical law. For Muslims, the various familiar biblical characters and the exploits with which they are traditionally associated are introduced instead into the Qur'an, the holy book of Islam. The Qur'an, however, represents much less familiar ground for a Western reader and, until comparatively recent times, was not generally available in English on the shelves of local bookstores. Non-Muslims may therefore be forgiven for imagining the Islamic faith to be something rather alien, particularly when its scripture is composed in what, for many, are the unintelligible squigglings of Arabic. Those who dip into an English translation of the Qur'an out of no more than casual curiosity will find chapters named after familiar biblical characters, including Abraham, Noah, Joseph, Jonah and Mary, mixed up with more arcane sounding titles like The Cow, The Bee and The Spider. Many people may be forgiven for wondering what it is all about.

Much of Islamic history may also appear to a Western eye to be a "grey area". The main obstacle to a better understanding probably lies, again, in what we are taught, or rather not taught. The curriculum in most schools in Europe and North America concentrates on the history of the last 2,000 years primarily from a European, then a Christian perspective. The Islamic record to a large extent involves neither, though over the centuries since its birth Islam has penetrated not only the Christian heartlands of Europe but also the Bible lands of Western Asia to an extent that not everyone readily appreciates. Much of Arab history took place in the Middle East and until much more modern times did not involve Western Europe or North America directly, though it did make its presence felt in the Far East and Africa. Until quite recently, particularly before the advent of the internet, the only sources of information about Islam for someone outside the faith were limited to academic libraries and specialist bookshops. Many of these works are written from a romanticized Muslim perspective that does not always respond faithfully to a more sanguine and objective view of history. Even today the workings of Islam are, in practice, foreign ground for many, since non-believers are not as a rule permitted to venture inside mosques and see what goes on with the freedom that allows tourists to stroll through Canterbury Cathedral or St Peter's basilica in Rome. One of the principal objections that many in Saudi Arabia had to American troops being stationed there during the Gulf War and, more recently, during the campaign in Afghanistan, lay in revulsion over the feet of infidels polluting holy ground. The southern and western part of the Arabian peninsula is the birthplace of Islam and the two most sacred cities of the faith, Mecca and Medina, lie within the borders of Saudi Arabia. Allegedly it was this intrusion, seen by fundamentalists as a sacrilege, which triggered Osama bin Laden to follow his catastrophic course.

For most of us the Islamic past amounts to little more than a two-dimensional canvas on which certain names and events are sketched without any seeming background, connection or purpose. We may know vaguely of a warrior called Saladin who once presented a formidable challenge to the Crusaders at Jerusalem.

We may just about have heard of warlords such as Suleyman the Magnificent and Tamerlane. We may have seen Genghis Khan riding his way through the celluloid fantasy version of events portrayed by Hollywood film moguls and Kublai Khan may or may not have had something to do with a place called Xanadu. Those of us who have visited Moorish Spain have perhaps cast a tourist's eye over the architectural magnificence of the Alhambra, scanned the guidebook and marvelled for a while before our return to the Costa and devotion to the important matter of bronzing. Few of us can claim to be authorities on Islamic history and its personalities.

Another element that might almost have been designed to cause confusion lies in the tortuous nature of history in the Middle East where Islam arose and maintained its real strength. At times this makes the story particularly difficult for the layman to follow. In much of the western hemisphere we have trodden, by comparison, a neat and tidy historical path through 2,000 years of Christendom. The Romans, the Anglo-Saxons and the Normans invaded Britain a long time ago whilst North America has only witnessed limited wars of independence. Western Europe may have been fought over more frequently but conflict has largely been amongst nation states of similar Christian persuasion. Not so the lands of Islam's birth whose geography has always made them a political melting pot. Arabia enjoys the dubious benefit of lying on a strategically and commercially sensitive crossroads between east and west, north and south. It forms the bridgehead between three continents, Europe, Asia and Africa. Since time immemorial he who controlled Western Asia could say that he controlled the world, since it provides a springboard to the countries of the Mediterranean, the Caucasus to the north, Africa to the south, India and the vast hinterlands of Central Asia to the north and east. The Middle East has thus been fought over, won, lost, raped, pillaged and plundered since people first realized the benefits of living there 7,000 years ago, in what has been justly called the Cradle of Civilization.

True to form, the 1,500 years or so of Islamic history have seen constant comings and goings of power-brokers from all quarters of the globe to do battle for possession of the Middle East. The rulers of various empires and would-be empires have cast a covetous eye on the region and been ready to claim it as their own. It has been squabbled over by Europeans, Persians, Mongols, Afghans, Turks, Abyssinians and, more recently, Americans anxious over the security of a wealth in the desert soil not recognized in the lifetime of Muhammad the Prophet, oil. Each stage of Islam's rather complicated history in the region and beyond is the focus of a separate chapter in this book, but it may help, at this state, to draw an outline sketch.

Before the birth of Muhammad, the founder of Islam, in the sixth century CE (the abbreviation of Current Era, the system of dating used throughout this book

Above: *A portrait by the 16th-century Italian artist Cristofano Altissimo of the great Muslim sultan Saladin (1138–1193), who fought successfully against the Christian crusaders.*

Above: *Medieval map of Arabia and India by Pedro Reinel, drawn in around 1519 and contained in the Miller Atlas.*

because it is more familiar to a Western reader than the Muslim calendar), two antique superpowers faced each other. To the West, with its headquarters in Constantinople (modern Istanbul in Turkey), was the surviving eastern wing of the much-weakened Roman Empire, named as the Byzantine Empire because Constantinople was formerly known as Byzantium. To the East in Persia (modern Iran) a dynasty known as the Sassanids ruled over a sizeable territory. In the western part of the Near East the Byzantines controlled roughly the area now covered by Israel, Lebanon, Jordan and Syria, extending from Palmyra in the north down as far as Petra. The Sassanids ruled over most of the Tigris and Euphrates valleys, old Mesopotamia, but neither the Byzantines nor the Sassanids laid claim to the area of desert in the southern half of the Arabian peninsula. This remained a somewhat lawless tribal region, run by local and generally despotic warlords, from whom the two empires recruited mercenaries to police remote borders and mount occasional raids. It had largely reverted to, or never converted from, paganism and it was here that Islam first found its inspiration and that Muhammad was able to find a potent seedbed for recruits to Islam.

The Islamic faith thus began in the Middle East and in the desert region of Mecca, Saudi Arabia, late in the sixth century. From there it was destined to spread south to Egypt and North Africa, advance west into the Iberian peninsula and east through Central Asia as far as China. At various times it ebbed and flowed north through the Caucasus into the Balkans and other parts of Europe.

The life of Muhammad is dealt with in a chapter of its own. After his death in 632 CE and the precarious establishment of the new religion in the south-west of the Arabian peninsula, the Muslim world was set to put down proper roots and to achieve rapid growth, partly through peaceable conversion, but largely through force of arms. In this respect the sentimental ideal that some Muslim writers would have their readers accept, that all took place by amicable persuasion, is simply untrue and even the Qur'an encourages a resort to force of arms if other approaches fail. The first period of growth, lasting for a little less than 30 years, may be compared with that of the patriarchs in Old Testament tradition. For the followers of Sunni Islam, the dominant movement, it represented a brief golden age and included the reigns of the so-called "Four Rightly Guided Caliphs": Abu Bakr, 'Umar, 'Uthman and 'Ali. These were not only the earliest evangelists of Islam after Muhammad, they were also fighting men who first took possession of Sassanid territory and then began a programme of conquest towards all points of the compass.

Expansion resulted in the establishment of two successive Islamic dynasties, the Umayyads and the Abassids. These families were maintained in power through tribal loyalties and the amassing of slave labour, much of which was put to work in the armed forces. The Umayyads, beginning with the Caliph Mu'awiya, ruled for a hundred years, consolidating control over much of the Middle East and made their power base in Damascus in Syria. They took a firm grip of parts of the Byzantine Empire and the Holy Land of Palestine, marched west along the coast of North

Below: A Turkish miniature painted at around the turn of the 17th century, by an unknown artist, depicts the prophet Muhammad observing the course of battle on Mount Uhrud during the earliest period of Islamic expansion.

Africa to the Atlantic and then advanced through Spain as far as southern France. Separately they went both north beyond the Caucasus, the range of mountains extending north-west from the Black Sea to the Caspian Sea, and east through Central Asia only halting at the Chinese border. Nowhere seemed particularly safe from the acquisitive eye of the Umayyad rulers. But their grip was destined to weaken, internal dissent mounted and in 750 CE another dynastic family came to power amid great bloodshed, resulting in the assassination of all the princely Umayyad families except one that escaped to Spain.

The Abassids were much less interested in expansionist policies than their predecessors but they were essentially a Persian-based Muslim culture rather than the Semitic one represented by the Umayyads. They abandoned Damascus as a capital and from a new centre of power in Baghdad they ruled the Islamic Empire for some 500 years until 1258 CE when the last of the caliphs was evicted from Iraq by a new, non-Muslim strongman from the East, Genghis Khan or Temujin. Having laid waste to more or less everything his Golden Horde set eyes upon from China to Russia, the Mongol Empire of the khans controlled most of the old Abassid Empire but was short-lived. A new period of Muslim history commenced with the rise of the Ottoman dynasty of Turks at the close of the thirteenth century. For 700 years the Ottoman Empire saw considerable ebb and flow in its fortunes, largely attributable to the differing policies and variable qualities of its leadership. It did, however, sustain and nurture the faith of Islam within its borders against various, mainly Christian pressures. One of its biggest early setbacks, however, arose in the face of attack mounted not by Christians, but from the East and by another Mongol Turk, Tamerlane, ironically himself a Muslim convert. It was not until after his death in Samarkand in 1405 CE that the Ottoman Empire was able to remarshal its strength and regain power over lands it had lost. The empire reached its peak in the sixteenth century under the leadership of Suleyman the Magnificent and then, in common with those that had gone before, began to wane. Its twilight years were coloured by a familiar roll-call of corrupt officials at the top, by ever-increasing fragmentation of its territories and by unwise military adventures.

The demise of the Ottomans did not arrest or weaken Islam since it was already widespread and well-established independently of state politics. Many of the Islamic republics and kingdoms emerged from the First World War with their own individual status and sovereignty and today Muslim communities are to be found worldwide, though still largely concentrated in and around the Arabic-speaking countries. However, Indonesian Muslims in the Far East not only constitute the majority, but also the largest Islamic population of any country in the world.

One of the most important measures to grasp for someone discovering Islam for the first time is that Islam is not just a religion. It is a total way of life dominated by religious beliefs, traditions and practices. As with Judaism and Christianity its origins have become blurred. Passage of time has tended to smudge the borders between myth and reality and much of the early tradition needs to be viewed with a degree of caution. In doing so, an objective historian always risks alienating the fundamentalist

Above: *The emperor Suleyman the Magnificent besieges Belgrade in this painting from 1543.*

believer, regardless of the nature of the religion. Perhaps nowhere is this more true than among Muslim communities where fundamentalism plays an important role and where the Qur'an is believed to contain divine and inalienable revelation directly from God. In this book I have attempted to steer a sensible and moderate path between that which is down to sheer faith and what is based on proven historical evidence.

The same road of moderation needs to be taken in respect of Muslim fundamentalism of the more aggressive nature that has constantly filled newspapers and TV screens since the events of 11 September 2001. To suggest that Islam, by nature, follows an aggressive doctrine is as superficial a view as to suggest that it does not! The majority of Muslims are peaceable people but aspects of Islamic behaviour in today's world are also undoubtedly militant and bloody. So, however, has been the conduct of Christian fanatics and Jewish zealots during the course of their respective histories. The appalling slaughter that took place in New York in pursuit of the extremist religious dogma proclaimed by Osama bin Laden, compares uncomfortably with the fanatical slaughter of tens of thousands of innocents in the south of France during the Fourth Crusade under the leadership of Simon de Montfort. Newspaper reports have suggested recently that the warlords in post-Taliban Afghanistan are keen to maintain styles of punishment for criminal behaviour including stoning, cutting off of hands and decapitation that many will feel are positively medieval and in places the Qur'an itself condones severe punishment when other methods of maintaining order fail. Yet not that long ago we were eager to burn

Below: A father and son read from the Qur'an together during a religious festival in Indonesia where about 90 percent of the population are Muslims.

fellow Christians at the stake on the most flimsy of evidence and more or less at the whim of clerics. When a member of the Women's Institute in the leafy suburbs of England sings that she "Will not cease from mental fight, nor shall my sword sleep in my hand", she may not be about to engage in actual sabre-rattling herself but is echoing a sentiment that, in the days of Kitchener of Khartoum, attacking the Muslim caliph at Omdurman in 1898, bore a more sanguine ring of truth. The reality is that Islam has been, and will continue to be, fertile ground for extremists, much as has been the experience in the history of other religious movements. If anything the difference of degree lies in age. As the youngest of the trio of monotheistic faiths, Islam often still burns with the fires of passion that have largely been reduced to smouldering embers in Christianity and Judaism. On this score the argument over who is more or less responsible for hostility and bloodshed between Jew and Muslim in the Middle East is outside the scope of this book.

In terms of its theology Islam differs essentially from Judaism and Christianity in that it views the holy prophet Muhammad (sometimes spelled Mahomet in English translation) as the divinely inspired messenger of Allah's will. It perceives Judaism as having become corrupted away from the faith of the patriarchs, the prophets who delivered the Word of God sincerely if incompletely before the time of Muhammad, and it views Jesus Christ not as a divine incarnation of God but as a mortal figure who was also empowered with the gift of prophecy. As far as the doctrine and practices of Christendom are concerned, it has to be said that Muhammad would appear to have been presented with only a very limited and perhaps distorted image of the Christian faith.

The word "Islam" is the infinitive form of an Arabic verb meaning "to submit" and fundamental to the belief of Islam is the understanding that humankind must bend totally to the will of God, delivered through Muhammad. The very name given to followers of the faith of Islam, Muslim (Moslem), is a word that in Arabic means "those who submit". Each person is an 'abd of God, a term that infers a blend of spiritual devotion called 'ibada, and physical day-to-day service, mu'amallat. So, in effect, what goes on in the market place and the mosque can never be separated. Islam is a "natural religion" in as much as everything in creation is seen to exist dependent upon God. It follows that obedience to and worship of God are paramount in life and one of the most tangible effects of this understanding is that politics and religion in the Islamic world cannot be separated. Today it has been calculated that Islam attracts approximately 1,000 million faithful worldwide though the figure is difficult to substantiate because in many countries claiming accountable Muslim populations there has been little or no effective census on which to base accurate numbers.

Readers may come across Arabic words describing people, events, items and practices that at first seem unfamiliar. Sometimes straightforward "translations" come to hand so a khalifa (Muslim ruler), translates conveniently into a caliph but it is not always this simple. There is no easy way, for example, to find an Anglicized one-word substitute to describe the qibla wall in a mosque, so it is a matter of becoming familiar with these terms, which are incorporated into the text in italics.

1 THE ORIGINS OF ISLAM

RELIGIOUS MOVEMENTS TEND NOT TO FORM IN A vacuum or as some blinding flash of passion. Their initial inspiration may come from one person within the span of a single lifetime but in their subsequent shaping and popular spread they amount to organic growths that rely on a gradual acceptance by people and governments. New religions usually draw on precedents found in other older faiths and they often arise in response to the need for change in social and cultural conditions. This may involve creating a new identity for a community or a fresh sense of purpose. During the course of history nowhere has this been more true than in the foundation of what eventually became known as Judaism, a religion born to provide a distinct cultural identity and raison d'etre for a hitherto loose assembly of nomads whose vision was to find a place to call their own. The other side of the coin is that existing religious movements tend to be at their most

vulnerable when there is strife and discontent. The most potent illustration in more recent times was the fall of Tsarist Russia at the beginning of the twentieth century when the popular uprising rejected the age-old Russian Orthodox religion that had become associated with corruption and oppression and willingly embraced communism. The rise of Islam falls closely into this pattern and many of the circumstances surrounding the foundation of Judaism and Christianity can also be found in the origins of Islam. They do much to explain its early successes.

Islamic inspiration rested directly in the exceptional and charismatic personality of Muhammad, born early in the sixth century CE, but the "seedbed" of the religion is a more ancient one and to understand it we need to glance into the past history of the Arabian peninsula and the surrounding nations of the Near and Middle East. Most Westerners brought up in a Jewish or Christian tradition will have learned something of how and why their own religious movements unfolded. There can be few people who have not heard of Moses, the Exodus from Egypt and the colonization of Syrio-Palestine as the promised "Holy Land". Every Christian knows the story of the Nativity of Jesus and remembers the severe impositions of Herodian rule from reading the Nativity story. Much less familiar will be the circumstances of Islam's birthplace, not least because the history of the Middle East between the time of Christ and the birth of Muhammad is mainly studied only by historians and scholars of the Orient.

As can be said of most faiths, the early traditions of Islam no doubt add up to a mixture of mythology and historical fact. It is sometimes impossible to distinguish one from the other because the origins of each and every faith have been carried in part by word of

Above: A mid-16th-century
copy of the World Map made
originally by the Islamic scholar
Al-Idris for Roger of Sicily in
1154. It covers the regions
familiar to Arab traders and
includes parts of Europe, Africa,
India, Indonesia and China.

Previous page: Ibrahim
(Abraham) preparing to sacrifice
his son. In Muslim tradition it is
not Isaac but Ishmael that he
intended to offer to God as a
token of his faith.

mouth and only later written down to become an "established truth". During this
time of oral tradition elements of myth and reality inevitably become blurred. The
Qur'an contains elements that fundamentalists see as divinely revealed truth to be
accepted word for word. Other theologians regard them as more symbolic while
the objective historian might argue that they amount to campfire stories that
served a good ideological purpose. Some of the elements of Islamic origins will be
familiar and the blending of fact and fable easy to recognize because Jews,
Christians and Muslims actually share common traditions about their ancestry,
one of the first surprises for an uninformed Westerner. According to both the
Bible and the Qur'an we all gained our vision of a universal and transcendent God
from the inspiration of Abraham.

According to the biblical book of Genesis, a work rooted in word-of-mouth
traditions and therefore largely difficult to verify, Abraham was the ancestor of
the Semitic peoples, whose confederation of twelve tribes was to become known
first as the Israelites then, after the return from exile in Babylon in 538 BCE, as
Jews. He is thought to have lived early in the second millennium BCE, probably
before 1800, although some historians place him as early as the Middle Bronze

Age around 2200 BCE. The early second millennium date does, however, best tie in with what is known of the population of the area to the east of the River Jordan or "Trans-Jordan" at the time and with archaeological evidence relating to the period of warfare that is described at the beginning of Genesis 14.

Muslims regard Abraham, known to them as Ibrahim, not only as the first of the great prophets of God but the father of the Arab peoples through his eldest son, Ishmael. The terms "Arab" and "Semite" have been greatly politicized but they are probably best thought of as different families of languages rather than in racial terms. In the modern world "Arab" refers strictly to Arabic-speaking people in parts of the world extending from Egypt and North Africa to South-West Asia, irrespective of whether or not they claim Arab descent. Several early writers claimed that Arab and Jewish peoples were all derived from the same root and the origin of this tradition must, ironically, be credited to the first-century Jewish writer, Josephus, who stated in his *Antiquities* that "the twelve sons of Ishmael conferred their names on the Arab nation and its tribes". Historically the Arabic-speaking peoples have been divided into two cultural groups. One includes the nomadic tribes of Bedouins, the other those more permanent communities living in the towns and oases. The two have not always seen eye to eye, however, and it is among the settled Arabs that the tradition of common ancestry with the Jewish stock largely developed. In the fifth century CE the historian Sozomenus wrote that some of the Arab tribes "happening to come into contact with the Jews, gathered from them the facts of their true origin, returned to their kinsmen, and inclined to the Hebrew customs and laws". Among the evidence is the fact that today both Muslims and Jews follow a number of common social practices and rituals such as circumcision.

Left: *An angel bearing a ram as the "scapegoat" appears before Ibrahim, the father of the Arab peoples, as he is about to sacrifice Ishmael to his God.*

As the first patriarch, Abraham is seen by all three faiths as a man of unstinting devotion to the universal deity, prepared to go to any lengths to meet the instructions of his God. It was into this discipline that he also trained Ishmael. The mother of Ishmael was Hagar, an Egyptian slave and concubine given to Abraham by his wife Sarai (Sarah) when she appeared to be barren. When she became pregnant, Hagar was humiliated by a jealous Sarai to the extent that she fled. But she was encouraged to return and gave birth to Ishmael when Abraham was in his 87th year. A little more than 10 years later, and after repeated prayers on Abraham's part to relieve his legitimate wife of lifelong barrenness, Sarai bore him a second son, Isaac. At this juncture Islamic tradition differs from that of Judaism and Christianity. Christians and Jews accept the Genesis story of how Abraham was prepared to sacrifice Isaac as a test of his faith in God. For Muslims it was not Isaac's life but that of the first-born son, Ishmael, that was demanded by Allah as a token of the faith of Ibrahim.

Because of Abraham's position as father of the Arab races, other patriarchal figures of the Old Testament are also recognized in the Qur'an and it is probably fair to say that the perception that a Muslim has of the roots of Islam compares closely with that found in the Bible about the beginnings of Judaism. Ibrahim is considered sufficiently important to be mentioned in greater or lesser detail in twenty-five *surahs* of the Qur'an. Other familiar common ground between the faiths includes the Genesis story of Adam and Eve's sojourn in the Paradise garden and of Eve's temptation by the devil, incidents that are described in the second *surah* of the Qur'an, *Al-Baqarah*. The same chapter also contains extensive reference to the part played by Moses in spreading his faith in the universal God. The twelfth *surah* includes a detailed account of the visit of Joseph to Egypt to buy corn and the Qur'an is peppered with other common traditions including those of Lot, Jonah, David, Solomon and Zacharias, all of whom are cast in the

roles of earlier prophets. Islamic legend maintains that Shem, the eldest son of Noah and therefore one of those who survived the Flood, migrated with his family to the region that became Syria and settled the land where the city of Damascus was to be founded. It was on account of this tradition that Damascus took on sacred significance for Muslims. Christians associate the city with the conversion of St Paul and the fact that he subsequently took refuge in the town. Jerusalem is important, of course, in the common tradition of all three faiths as a holy city and Muhammad being carried there in his mystical and visionary experience included Muslims in this mutual belief.

Right: A map preserved in the mosaic floor of a church dating from the 6th century CE at Madaba in Jordan, provides some of the most accurate information about how the city of Jerusalem appeared during the Byzantine era.

Islam, therefore, is rooted in a common ancestral tradition of people who kept faith with the same omnipotent and universal God, whether they called him El, Yahweh or Allah. So what brought Muslims to go their separate ways and, incidentally, what caused the varying degrees of Islamic antagonism towards Jews and Christians that are seen in the world today?

In part the divergence is due to ideological differences that developed over the course of time, but much can also be put down to secular politics and armed struggle. For thousands of years before the birth of Islam the Middle East had been a melting pot of different cultures, with nations coming and going in successive waves of conquest and people migrating from place to place. Tensions were always exacerbated by the fact that the region serves as a geographical hub between East and West. It is where many roads meet and it has always been a strategic focus for trade and power politics alike. Aside from the fairly inhospitable Hijaz region, largely arid desert though with significant oases and wells where the cities of Mecca, Medina and a few others were to be founded, the area of southern and western Arabia included the Yemen, Bahrain and Oman, parts of which were fairly affluent from about 1000 BCE onwards. The farmers of the Yemen grew abundant crops, camel trains across the desert became fairly sophisticated operations and the tribes of the region benefited from increased trade with wealthy Mediterranean cities such as Petra in Jordan and Palmyra in Syria. Regular caravans plied the frankincense route to Gaza and it was with one of these that a famous Sabaean (Sheban) queen probably travelled to play upon the heartstrings of King Solomon.

To understand the background to Islam we need to tread the historical path from before the time of Jesus Christ when much of the region was effectively dominated by the Roman Empire, to a very different era when Muhammad was born some 650 years later. The intervening centuries had seen momentous changes to the political and religious map of the area. At the dawn of the Christian era the Mediterranean world and most of the Near East, including Egypt, Palestine and the whole of Asia Minor, were controlled by the imperial legions and administered from an all-powerful Rome. Facing the eastern wing of the Roman Empire was the only other major imperial power in the area, that of Persia. The region from which modern Saudi Arabia was eventually to emerge was, in part, termed a dependent or client state, although in the second and third centuries CE "Arabia", as it became known, was effectively a Roman province made up of several adjacent regions that had been ruled by the old kingdom of Nabataea.

We know very little about the Nabataeans other than a limited sketch from the period of the third century BCE. They are part of the prehistory of the area and they seem to have been a nomadic people who originated somewhere in the north-west hinterland of Arabia. In the fourth century BCE they settled in the south-eastern region of the area to the east of the River Jordan, named Trans-Jordan in 1916 by the League of Nations when the mandate for its control was given to Britain. The Nabataeans were attracted by the commercial benefits of a life beside the major caravan routes from Arabia to the Mediterranean and they founded the awesome rock-hewn city of Petra in southern Jordan as their capital. From the third century

Left: *Rock tombs at Petra in Jordan, the capital of the Nabataean desert kingdom between the 3rd century* BCE *and the 1st century* CE, *built by nomads after opting for a more settled lifestyle.*

BCE Petra was a great trading centre until superseded in the second millennium CE by the Syrian city of Palmyra, which also bridged a major trade route between East and West. The importance of Petra was at an end in 106 CE when Roman emperor Trajan stormed the city and took over the Nabataean territories, incorporating them into the Arabian province that included all lands bordering the Red Sea, Sinai, the Negev desert and the plain of Moab.

From the time of Christ, Rome had been expanding her territories eastward step by step, more or less without resistance. The notable exception was the empire of the Parthians, a Persian-based dynasty that had seized control of large parts of Mesopotamia in the second century BCE, breaking away from the Greek-speaking

Above: *A stone relief depicting Roman Praetorian Guards, dating from the 2nd century CE.*

Seleucids who had dominated it previously. The Parthians who came to oversee these lands fought a particularly vicious war against the Roman legions between 162 and 166 CE and they were not eliminated as a significant political and military force until 224 CE. On the eastern seaboard of the Mediterranean, in Palestine, Jerusalem was in ruins after the momentous siege by Roman forces in 70 CE and the Jewish peoples had been dispersed all over the area, including Arabia, a not insignificant factor in the subsequent rise of Islam.

Thus the situation remained until early in the third Christian century, which saw the rise of another aggressive Persian dynasty, keen to challenge Roman supremacy. These were the Sassanids who galvanized Persia into a new sense of nationalistic fervour from their power base in the city of Pars and proclaimed the intention of recovering the entire empire that had been held by their ancestors, the Achaemenids. These were the original Persian empire-builders who, under Cyrus the Great, had released the Israelites from their incarceration in Babylon some 200 years before the arrival of Alexander the Great in 323 BCE. In the third century CE long and savage wars erupted between the two superpowers, during which Rome steadily lost territory to the Persians. The first attack on Roman colonies came in the years between 230 and 232 CE under the leadership of the founding Sassanid ruler, Ardashir. A Roman historian of the period, Cassius Dio, drew a stark picture: "He (Ardashir) was indeed a source of fear to us, menacing not only Mesopotamia and Syria but threatening to regain everything that the ancient Persians had occupied, as being an ancestral possession" (Dio, *Roman History* 80. 3).

Other advances were soon to follow and everywhere in the East the legions of Rome fell back until the Emperor Valerian himself was taken prisoner by the second Persian ruler Shapur I in 260 during the next Persian invasion of Mesopotamia (modern Iraq). Shapur's conquests were then extended as far as Palestine, aided

along the way by the poorer sections of the communities he overran, people who
had suffered punitive taxation and other social hardships under Roman occupation
and were keen to see them sent packing.

The Persians followed neither the monotheistic religion of the Christians nor
the polytheism of the Roman legions, which were still firmly attached to paganism,
but a faith peculiar to themselves, Zoroastrianism. The prophet Zoroaster, its
founder and arguably the earliest prophet known to have existed, is widely
accepted to have lived in about the fifteenth century BCE although other traditions
place his birth at any time between 6000 BCE and 600 BCE. Over a period of a
thousand years three successive Persian empires had followed Zoroastrianism as
their state religion. The first dynasty known to have embraced the faith were the
Achaemenids, followed by Parthians and finally the Sassanids, the last of whose
rulers, Yazdegird, died in exile in 652 CE, having been forced to flee Persia by
advancing Muslim forces.

Zoroastrianism has exerted more influence on Judaism, Christianity and Islam
than is generally recognized. Zoroaster claimed that he had received revelations
from God, who he knew as Ahura Mazda, the source of light in the world and the
omnipotent creator of all that is good. Opposing Ahura Mazda stood Angra
Mainyu, the alter ego of the god of light, representing darkness, violence, evil and
death. It was Zoroaster who taught the importance of free will in deciding man's
fate in the after-life and who introduced ideas such as the existence of heaven and
hell and the resurrection of the body.

The history and religions of northern Arabia and the lands beyond is thus reasonably clear, if not exactly straightforward. In its southern half, however, the Arabian peninsula had always been less well defined politically and culturally. Southern and western Arabia, including the area known as the Hijaz in which one finds the holy cities of Mecca and Medina and from which Muhammad recruited most of his support, largely remained outside of any Roman or Persian influence. Much of the area of the Arabian peninsula consists of desert and flat, arid grassland or steppe punctuated by occasional oases and watering places. Only in the far south-west, where the climatic conditions are less severe, do fertile and well-watered valleys allow farming to be carried on effectively.

The city of Mecca (sometimes written as Bakkah or Makkah) lies about 80 kilometers east of the shore of the Red Sea and is claimed by some historians to be within easy reach of the old caravan routes connecting Jeddah, Yemen and Palestine. The city rests in a basin surrounded on all sides by chains of mountains running from north to south and originally it may have served as a halt on the caravan trails, though this is disputed. According to some theorists the small settlement that arose there may have been developed because of its well. This served to make it a convenient meeting place for merchant travellers to barter goods, though what these goods would have been is not clear. Whatever the circumstances surrounding the foundation of Mecca, legend credits Ishmael with having been the first person to settle there permanently.

There are problems with the traditional version of history, not least because Mecca lies at the bottom of a barren valley that would not necessarily have been inviting for caravans to visit, particularly when the more accessible city of Ta'if was nearby. The earliest firm reference to a place called Mecca comes from a manuscript known as the *Continuatio Byzantia Arabica* written during the rule of the Umayyad *khalifa* Hisham (724–43 CE). No written evidence of any reliability occurs before that period, although a doubtful reference by the Alexandrian geographer Ptolemy in the second century CE mentions a place called Makoraba, without offering any further clue that this and Mecca might be one and the same. It has been argued in recent years that Mecca could not possibly have been sited near to a major trade route, nor did it amount to a significant stopping off point on an east–west, north–south crossroads because it lies more or less on the edge of the peninsula.

An additional puzzle of a different kind has emerged from archaeological discoveries at the sites of some early Egyptian mosques. These indicate quite clearly that, as late as the early part of the eighth century CE, Muslims were angling the direction of their prayers not in the direction of Mecca but somewhere further to the north. A number of excavations at other North African mosques of the period apparently reveal a *qibla* wall facing south, while in Jordan excavations reveal the *qibla* direction occasionally to be north, in both circumstances facing away from Mecca. A number of archaeologists now believe that the earliest sanctuary was not in the south-west of Arabia at all but either in the north-west or even further north, in which case Jerusalem becomes a strong contender. Interestingly Greek trading documents of the seventh century CE sometimes refer to Ta'if and Yathrib (Medina) but make no mention of Mecca, which would seem to conflict with the claim that it was a major and affluent trade centre.

As time went on, the region of southern Arabia saw the rise of a number of small city-states holding ancient tribal loyalties. The most senior of these was Saba, better known to anyone familiar with the Old Testament as Sheba. In the seventh and sixth centuries BCE the Sabaeans controlled a sizeable empire from their capital at Marib, stretching from the city of Nagran in the north-west to the Indian Ocean in the east and to Abyssinia (Ethiopia) in the south. Much of this kingdom, however, was to become eroded by other tribes vying for supremacy, most notably the Qatabanians and Hadramites. Many of the tribes involved in these ebbs and flows of power play had almost certainly emigrated from the north in prehistoric times and had brought with them the rudiments of civilization. Neither the Romans nor the Sassanid Persians were able to annexe their lands and, although the Greeks might have done so in their time of glory, the opportunity was lost to them because of the untimely death of Alexander the Great. So the southern half of Arabia amounted to a frontier zone bordering lands outside the control of either of the two competing imperial powers. Within this rather lawless interior of occasional settlements, camel tracks and some armed border posts sponsored by either the Byzantines or the Sassanids, groups of insurgents roamed freely and they became loosely known as "Saracens", a term coined apparently to identify any small federations of warring Arabs. The situation was about to change however.

The tribes may not have been under either Persian or Roman control but the strength of trade brought these southern Arabs into regular contact with the outside world from about 400 CE onwards. Furthermore the great powers, though unable to control them effectively, were certainly willing to make use of them. The tribes occupied what amounted to a buffer zone and mercenaries from among the southern tribes were employed by both sides to act as frontier guards and, at the same time, to make life difficult for the opposition by mounting regular cross-border sorties.

In terms of religious belief, the city-states that eventually arose in the south and west of the peninsula amounted to a veritable melting pot. Because the position was of trading importance their populations became highly cosmopolitan as different commercial enterprises took up residence. Christians and Jews rubbed shoulders with people who adhered to old tribal faiths in a pantheon of gods and goddesses, particularly in areas like the Yemen and around Medina, and a fairly easy arrangement of live and let live was maintained. Records from one town, Najran in

the south-west, indicate that it was ruled by a Jewish king but sustained a prominent Christian religious administration. At least one tribe, the Hanifs, appear to have adopted a style of monotheistic religion independent of any other. Whether or not it amounted to some vestige of the monotheism allegedly brought by Abraham and Ishmael in antiquity is impossible to tell. What does seem clear is that, in the main, polytheism was the order of the day for people in the Hijaz region. This is supported by tradition in the biography of Muhammad, which describes how his new Islamic followers in Mecca cleansed the focus of pre-Islamic worship, the Ka'aba, of its stock of idols. Much of the old religious practice may indeed have been abhorrent to Muslims, but some aspects were actually retained. These included respect for special holy times of the year, including the month of Ramadan, when fighting ceased and precise rituals had to be followed. The practice of making pilgrimage to sacred places, one of which was to Mecca and the sanctuary known as the Ka'aba, was already important.

Whatever the nature of its origins, Mecca had almost certainly seen its beginnings as a small village settlement that had later been taken over and expanded by the Quraysh tribe of Arabs. The Ka'aba claims a curious tradition for which we need to return briefly to the biography of Ibrahim (Abraham). The biblical narratives indicated that Ibrahim and his tribe came originally from Ur in southern Mesopotamia and that he emigrated from there because of the threat of armed incursion by people known as Amorites. He made a trek of some 800 kilometres north and west and resettled in the town of Haran where he lived with his wife, Sarai, until he was about 75 years of age. He then packed his bags again, migrating into the coastal country of Canaan, bisected by the River Jordan. Here he stayed long enough to see his God rectify the shortcomings among the people of Sodom and Gomorrah before heading south towards the Negev region. When famine broke out there he went on to Egypt with his family and befriended the Pharaoh before returning to Canaan.

Conflicting traditions emerge concerning exactly who built the Ka'aba, when and under what circumstances. One story indicates that at some stage during his wanderings, and in the company of his son Ishmael, Ibrahim found himself in the Hijaz region of southern Arabia and decided to build a shrine to his personal god as he had done in various other places such as Beer-Sheba. He and Ishmael gathered crude blocks of stone from the surrounding desert, including one massive black monolith, and they used the materials to construct a simple square sanctuary, which became known as the Ka'aba, meaning "a cube". Another version of events describes how continuing jealousy between Ishmael's mother, Hagar, and Sarai before her miraculous conception of Isaac obliged Ibrahim to separate the two women. He took Hagar and Ishmael to the well in the Meccan valley and left them to spend the remainder of their lives there. It was, therefore, Ishmael alone who built the Ka'aba. In time the place would become the foundation for the city of Mecca and it is believed that, for many hundreds of years before it was taken over by the Nabataeans and their successors for use in polytheistic

Opposite: *Rocky arid surroundings typical of the landscape in which the holy city of Mecca was founded.*

devotions, the Ka'aba was a place of worship for the arcane monotheistic cult that Abraham or Ishmael had left to posterity.

Towards the end of the third century CE control of southern Arabia lay in the hands of two new factions. In the west the Sabaeans and another tribal group known as the Himyars had joined forces in an alliance known as the Sabaean–Himyaric Empire. To the east the Hadramites, who now established their own expanded kingdom to rival the Sabaeans and their allies, had ousted the once dominant Qatabanians. This position proved no more stable than any of the previous ones because soon afterwards the Himyaric King Sammar Yuharis attack-ed and conquered the Hadramite kingdom. In doing so Sammar Yuharis forged the first single empire known to have existed in southern Arabia. Occasional attempts were made subsequently by disaffected tribes to break free from the arrangement but none succeeded and the empire was steadily expanded until it reached its peak of power under King Abukarib Assad in the early part of the fifth century CE. The situation was, however, destined to be short-lived.

Abukarib Assad's successor, Yusuf As, was responsible for a bloody incident that shifted the balance of power yet again. Yusuf As had adopted the Jewish faith and he chose to launch a campaign of repression against Abyssinians and Christians living in southern Arabia. The predominantly Christian town of Nagran was put under siege and eventually many of its inhabitants were massacred. This outrage triggered a military backlash from Abyssinia, supported by the forces of the Byzantine emperor in the north. A pitched battle was fought during which Yusuf As was killed and his forces comprehensively defeated, with the consequence that southern Arabia became an Abyssinian province. Administrative control of the area passed to a former Abyssinian general named Abreha who then proclaimed himself king in about 547 CE.

Meanwhile beyond the frontiers of southern Arabia, particularly in the north and west, history had been taking a different course, one to which the south was not to remain immune. Under Constantine the Great at the beginning of the fourth century, the seat of Roman secular power had shifted to Byzantium, which was renamed as the city of Constantinople in 330 CE and shortly afterwards the Roman Empire adopted Christianity as its official religion through an edict made by one of Constantine's immediate successors, Theodosius II. After the conquest of the city of Rome in 410 by the Visigoths under Alaric, from their European heartlands, the western wing of the Roman Empire was effectively at an end, though Byzantines maintained power over the east as the Christianized Holy Roman Empire. The Arab conquest of the seventh century began to erode their position but before this time the Byzantine Christians were constantly rivalled and harassed by the Persians. At first the forces of the Byzantines, under their general, Maurice, had made sweeping advances against the Sassanids and in the spring of 591 CE a so-called "everlasting peace" treaty was agreed between Constantinople and Persia. Though the alliance was to be short-lived the Sassanid king, Chosroes II, became an ally of the emperor.

At this stage of history and during the childhood of Muhammad, there was one more twist in the story affecting southern Arabia. The Abyssinian colonial ruler and self-styled king, Abreha, launched an abortive military strike against the Persians in the north. With the Abyssinians weakened a pro-Persian group active in the Yemen saw the opportunity to undermine Abyssinian control over the region and their emissaries secretly made contact with the Persians. Seeing a strategic opportunity opening up, Chosroes II sent an expeditionary force south and, with the support of Arab tribes, threw the Abyssinians out of Yemen so that, in effect, it became a new Persian enclave. Between 597 and 598 Chosroes II extended his grip on southern Arabia through another armed Sassanid incursion and the whole area then became a Persian province ruled by a governor known as a *satrap*.

The beginning of the seventh century saw the Persians advancing once more in the north. Chosroes II took the Christian city of Antioch in 613. In the following year, for the second time the Persian armies stood at the borders of Palestine and at this stage the remnants of Jewish population, seeing the way the tide of conquest was running, prudently joined forces with them against the Christians. Syria and Armenia fell to the Sassanids in short order and in the

Below: *This 19th-century engraving depicts a cavalry charge of Persians against the Christian forces.*

spring of 614 the Persian forces handed Jerusalem back to Jews who promptly took over all the Christian churches and expelled their members from the country. By 625 the Sassanid armies were encamped on the shores of the Bosphorus with Constantinople in their sights.

During this time of Persian success, however, the Byzantine Emperor Heraclius was restoring his military strength. Constantinople was put under siege but did not fall, largely because the defenders were successful in the use of "Greek Fire", the tactic of throwing boiling tar from the ramparts on to the attacking forces below. Eventually Heraclius embarked on a counter-offensive, which saw the restoration of Jerusalem to the Christians in March 629. Prior to this the Persian dynasty had controlled an area from Afghanistan and Pakistan in the north, and to the west, as we have discovered, as far as Palestine. Much of the area to the east of the Red Sea, including large parts of northern Arabia, also remained under Sassanid control.

It is against this tumultuous and confused backdrop of armies moving hither and thither across the landscape of the Middle East and of a hotch-potch of religious beliefs mingling together without any real cohesion or spiritual direction that matters were destined to change once more. During the eighth and ninth centuries the old imperial dynasties of Byzantium and Persia were to wane with the rise of popular support for Muhammad and the forces of Islam. The Sassanid Zoroastrians were destined for relegation to remote backwaters of the country, where they were given an inferior status and many were forced to live in poverty. The Roman imperial capital of Constantinople and its Byzantine Empire would exist for almost another thousand years, yet it was constantly threatened and ultimately forced to retreat before an army serving God by another name. It fell to the Turks in 1453 and was renamed Istanbul.

It was into this fraught political and religious arena that Muhammad was born in the mid-sixth century. Abyssinian colonialism had permitted a feudal system of domination by powerful warlords who inflicted considerable social injustice on the poorer classes and also kept them in check. This was accompanied by loss of community structure, inadequate maintenance of irrigation systems resulting in crop failures and diminishing trade. The cosmopolitan nature of the various clans and immigrants living side by side also meant that a plethora of religious beliefs nudged up to one another, including Judaism, Christianity, Zoroastrianism and tribal polytheism. All these things contributed to social discontent and a yearning for something better. It provided a seedbed for change and a situation that bears considerable similarity to the position of the Jews in Palestine in the century that witnessed the birth of Christ.

2 THE LIFE OF MUHAMMAD, THE HOLY PROPHET

THE MAIN MISSION OF THE PROPHET MUHAMMAD WAS ONE OF EVANGELISM. His intention was to rid southern Arabia of polytheism and to restore the monotheistic belief that he believed had been revealed by earlier prophets from the time of Abraham but then corrupted. This restoration of the true faith revealed to him, the last of the prophets, was to be accompanied by the no less important reinstatement of the laws of God. It has to be said at the outset that biographical traditions about the Prophet are not always consistent. This is hardly surprising given that many of the details must have originated as word-of-mouth stories and recollections that gradually became established as fact and were eventually written down, often by chroniclers long after the death of

Muhammad. In this book I have attempted to provide as many of them as possible without distinction on grounds of historical credibility.

In the sense understood by Muslims a prophet is one who brings the word of God to humanity. The Islamic terms including *nabi* and *rasul* literally mean "a messenger" so that the two words, prophet and messenger, are more or less synonymous. The Qur'an in fact admits to the existence of many earlier prophets including Abraham and Moses from the Hebrew scripture, John the Baptist and Jesus Christ from the Christian New Testament. Thus Islamic doctrine does not claim that Muhammad was unique in his prophethood other than in the sense that, while prophets may have existed throughout history, he represents the "end of the line", the ultimate deliverer of divine revelation.

Muhammad was born into the highly respected and influential Quraysh tribe in either 569 or 570 CE in Mecca, which tradition claims to have been an ancient trading centre in the province of Al Hijaz, lying in the western part of the Arabian peninsula. His father, 'Abdullah, came from a somewhat impoverished branch of the tribe, the Hashim family. Stories of the history of the Quraysh are impossible to verify but they describe a member of the tribe named Qusayy marrying the daughter of a neighbouring tribal chieftain, Hulayl, whose clansmen at one time controlled Mecca and were the guardians of the Ka'aba. On his death Hulayl controversially chose that Qusayy should take over authority in preference to any of his own sons. In consequence and in order to safeguard his own position Qusayy encouraged his immediate kinsmen from the Quraysh tribe to settle and farm the valley lands immediately surrounding Mecca. They became known as the "Quraysh of the Hollow" to distinguish them from other members of the tribe

Above: *The birth of a Prophet witnessed by Aminah, Muhammad's mother.*

Opposite: *A map of the Red Sea area including the towns of Mecca and Medina from a late 12th-century Arabian manuscript atlas by Al Idrisi.*

who followed in their wake and settled in the surrounding hills and some of the valleys lying beyond. Qusayy fathered four sons and, on his death, 'Abd ad-Dar the eldest, assumed the mantle of authority. But he proved ineffectual and unpopular while Qusayy's second son, 'Abd Mandaf, was considered the better potential leader. The situation remained unchanged during 'Abd Mandaf's lifetime but when Hashim, his first-born son, reached maturity Hashim was backed by about half of the Quraysh families with the remainder supporting the succession of 'Abd ad-Dar. The two branches of the Quraysh were never to be fully reconciled. Hashim took a wife named Salma who bore him three sons, one of whom was Shaybah, better known in popular Islamic legend as 'Abd al-Muttalib since the story goes that one of Hashim's brothers, Muttalib, took his young nephew on a visit to Mecca where he was mistaken for Muttalib's slave. The derogatory title "'Abd al-Muttalib" means "servant of Muttalib" and although the misunderstanding was corrected by his uncle, Shaybah earned an affectionate nickname that stuck. 'Abd al-Muttalib, whose eldest son was 'Abdullah, was Muhammad's grandfather.

'Abdullah died in Yathrib (Medina) a few weeks before Muhammad was born and responsibility for the infant and his mother Aminah passed to his paternal grandfather, 'Abd al-Muttalib, already an important leader of the Quraysh tribe. Conflicting traditions claim that Muhammad was either raised in Medina by 'Abd al-Muttalib or, according to tribal custom, he was placed in the care of a Bedouin foster mother with whom his first years were to be spent in the desert. At the age of 6 his true mother is said to have taken him to Medina to visit his father's tomb. Aminah, however, died suddenly on the return journey, leaving Muhammad an orphan. He got safely back to Mecca but discovered that his grandfather had also passed away and so he was raised from the age of 8 by a generous if not particularly affluent uncle, Abu Talib. Due to the shortage of family income, the young Muhammad was obliged to work and so he became a shepherd boy earning a living amongst some of Abu Talib's farming neighbours. There is passing reference to Muhammad accompanying his uncle on at least one trade caravan to Bostra in Syria at the age of 10 or 12 and another report that Abu Talib established a shop in Mecca at which he may have helped out.

Tradition paints a picture of Muhammad as a shy and thoughtful young man who developed strong ethical principles early in life. He became popularly known as al-Ameen, an accolade meaning "honest" and "reliable", and his character seems to have been regarded as unimpeachable by Meccans and visitors alike. One reference implies that he was occasionally subject to attacks of epilepsy but this may have been a crude attempt to discredit the mystical experiences that were to

come. Like many of the Quraysh tribe he became a merchant when he reached maturity and his trading activities not only found him regularly at commercial fairs in Mecca and other Arabian towns, but appear to have taken him further abroad on expeditions to various parts of the Middle East including Syria. His professional work inevitably must have brought him into contact with those of other faiths including Christians and it is said that some of their doctrinal beliefs caused him concern.

At the age of 25 a major new influence had entered his life. He had built his reputation in Mecca as an honest broker and reports of integrity reached the ears of a wealthy widow named Khadija. She was seeking someone trustworthy to manage her business affairs and she employed Muhammad. The relationship grew and Khadija proposed marriage. According to conflicting reports, she was either 28 or 40, though the former may be more plausible since it is recorded that she gave birth to six children with Muhammad, two sons and four daughters. His first son Qasim died at the age of two and the second, 'Abdullah, also died in infancy. The four daughters were Zainab, Ruqayya, Umm Kulthum and Fatima. The first three died and Fatima alone survived.

Little more is known of this early period of the Prophet's life beyond the fact that he continued as a trader. Isolated biographical details mention that he attended the commercial fair of Hubashah in Yemen and the early Muslim writer, Ibn Hanbal describes him visiting the 'Abd al-Qais, thought to refer to the great fair of Daba in Oman. Contemporary Arab historians described this as a meeting place for traders from China, India, Persia and from the West, assembling there every year from far-flung parts of the globe. There is also mention of someone named Sa'ib who seems to have been a business partner of Muhammad at Mecca and who placed considerable trust in Muhammad's integrity. "We relied on each other; if Muhammad led the caravan, he did not enter his house on his return to Mecca without clearing accounts with me; and if I led the caravan, he would enquire about my welfare on my return and speak nothing about his own capital entrusted to me."

Muhammad's first taste of social reform came, not on his own account, but through a kinsman named Zuhair. It was not uncommon in Mecca for visiting traders to find themselves underpaid against previously agreed prices and on one occasion this resulted in a Yemeni composing a poem satirizing unscrupulous Meccan business ethics. The Yemeni trader was victimized and made the object of vilification, a response that deeply offended Zuhair who considered the poem entirely justifiable. He founded a caucus of fellow tribal leaders who agreed on an order of fair commercial practice, called *Hilf al-fudul*. Its charter was to give support to the oppressed in Mecca, irrespective of whether they were citizens or visiting foreigners. Muhammad joined the organization, attracted by its high principles, and later in his life he is said to have sharply defended his membership. "I have participated in it, and I am not prepared to give up that privilege even against a herd of camels; if somebody should appeal to me even today, by virtue of my pledge of loyalty, I shall hurry to his help."

Sparse detail is recorded from this period about Muhammad's religious orientation. It is maintained that he never became involved in idolatry, although he did come into close contact with the Ka'aba, the religious sanctuary in the centre of Mecca then used as a place of pagan worship, stocked according to tradition with 360 idols. It is noted that in about 605 the building was severely damaged by fire and then further weakened by flash floods so that it required substantial repair. A nice story arose that Muhammad joined fellow citizens in the rebuilding programme and that an argument developed about where the famous Black Stone, said to have been incorporated by the original builder, Abraham, should be relaid. Muhammad was called upon to arbitrate the dispute and ruled that whoever could lift the stone earned the right to position it. All tried and failed but Muhammad raised it with ease and placed it in the corner of the wall from which the Muslim religious perambulations at the time of the *hajj* were destined to start.

It is also mentioned that Muhammad had begun to emulate the practice of his grandfather in retiring to an isolated spot about 5 kilometres from Mecca on the slopes of Jabal-an-Nur, the "Mountain of Light", also known as Mount Hira, the "Mount of Revelation", where he would stay for periods of time in a small cave, particularly through the month of Ramadan, using the quiet sense of isolation to meditate and to pray for guidance from God. Today the cave has been accorded the title Ghar-i-Hira.

Left: *A delightful 16th-century miniature details the Ka'aba, the holiest Islamic shrine in Mecca.*

It was during one of these sojourns towards the end of Ramadan in about 610, after he had been visiting the cave for five years and as he approached middle age, that he witnessed the first of a series of visitations from the angel Jibril (Gabriel). In much the same manner that this celestial being had announced the impending birth of a messiah to Mary the mother of Jesus, he informed Muhammad that he was to be blessed with the gift of prophecy and was to be the messenger of Allah. He was taught how to perform ritual washing, how to pray and how to conduct the proper rites. Above all he was taught the art and importance of recitation as a means of coming close to God.

> *Recite in the name of your Lord who created – created man from clots of blood.*
> *Recite! Your Lord is Most Bountiful One, who by the pen taught man what he did not know.*
>
> (Qur'an: Al-'Alaq 96. 1–5)

Some traditions indicate that the revelations then ceased for a period of three years but eventually they resumed on Muhammad's subsequent visits to the desert retreat and were maintained there and elsewhere for the rest of Muhammad's life over a span of twenty-three years. It is said that the revealed verses were memorized before being recorded on a variety of available materials, such as leather, palm leaves, bark and animal bones and that they were recited in his daily prayers. Gradually, with the support and dedication of his wife, his friend Abu Bakr and

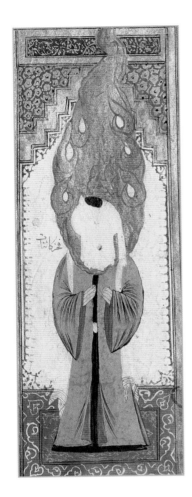

Above: *Detail of the prophet Muhammad at prayer.*

his cousin 'Ali, Muhammad had begun to accept that the visitations did not amount to some diabolic influence and that his mission in life was not only to be a prophet of the divine truth but the last of all the prophets. He accepted the existence of an absolute yet personal god in a part of the world where polytheism, the worship of many gods and goddesses, still dominated the religious scene. He also came to an implacable belief in the notion that the world as it was known would end with a Day of Judgement followed by resurrection for true believers. Eventually he gained sufficient confidence in his role to start reciting the revelations he had received to others and, with financial help from his wife, he gained a small following of about 50 adherents that included some leading citizens in Mecca and his own kinsmen, most notably his wife, his ally Abu Bakr who was to become the first *khalifa* and his servant Zayd ibn Harithah. Personal dedication to the new faith was summed up in the daily declaration, "There is no deity worthy of worship except Allah, the one true God and Muhammad is the messenger of Allah."

Not all approved of such radical ideology however. Mecca's alleged position as a key trading centre in the Middle East had brought prosperity to some of its citizens in unequal measure and his teachings, including calls for social reform, went down less than favourably with many of the rich and powerful merchant families. Muhammad was advocating such unpopular moves as better treatment for the underprivileged — slaves, women and orphans. He also began to urge loyalty to his Islamic faith over and above that of clan and tribal affiliations and in preference to the paganism that had held sway for hundreds of years as an ancestral faith. Antagonism towards him was not long in making itself felt and the hostility emanated not from other leaders in Mecca but from Muhammad's own Quraysh tribe, most notably from the clan of his uncle, Abu Lahab. At first the most vulnerable members of his following were picked out for harassment and there are indications that some were tortured and killed. Slaves were singled out and the first victim is said to have been a women by the name Umm Ammar. Muslims from the more affluent families were put under what amounted to house arrest, with the condition that only if they recanted would freedom of movement be restored.

Muhammad was forced at one stage to organize an evacuation out of the country to a more secure haven where moderation prevailed. Records indicate that in 615 he sent 83 families to neighbouring Ethiopia (Abyssinia) for their own safety. The country's ruler Ashabah, also known as Negus, was a Christian with a reputation of tolerance. Although the refugees departed from Mecca in small groups hoping to avoid detection, the Quraysh leaders discovered the escape and sent a deputation to Negus requesting their forcible repatriation. Negus declined the request.

Tragedy struck Muhammad four years later in 619 at the age of 50, when his only wife and the uncle who had raised him to manhood both died. As was the convention amongst Arabs Muhammad was to marry several other women. The first of these included Sawda, a 50-year-old widowed devotee, and 'A'isha, the daughter of Abu Bakr, in an arrangement that continued for about six years. Later in life he

Left: *Muslims at prayer around the sacred Ka'aba in Mecca whilst being threatened by pagan forces of the Quraysh tribe. Detail from a medieval Turkish manuscript.*

contracted to marry again and also took a Christian slave as a concubine. Despite earlier personal losses his embryo ministry continued to grow and with it the degree of opposition in Mecca to his brand of evangelism.

By 622 the antagonism had risen to such a dangerous level, with threats mounting against his own life, that he was forced to leave the city. Narratives suggest that he tried ineffectually to persuade the leaders of various tribes to support his cause. The Meccan authorities then issued an ultimatum to the Quraysh tribe to hand over Muhammad for summary execution. When they refused the tribe was boycotted and the ban lasted for three years. Another tradition records that a compromise was reached wherein Meccans were allegedly allowed the freedom of Islamic worship and pagan idolatry side by side after it was discovered that the documents recording the original boycott and stored in the Ka'aba had been attacked by ants and eaten away. The only words left untouched were those of the opening sentence, "In Your name, O Allah."

At this stage, however, Muhammad's departure from Mecca was unavoidable and the flight into exile with his followers in September 622 became known as the *hijrah* or *hegira*. It marks the opening year of the Islamic calendar. In all Muslim countries 622 CE is regarded as year 1 for religious purposes. The Muslim year is formulated on lunar months, thus there are about 103 Muslim years to 100 in the Gregorian calendar, which is based on solar years. The cycle is corrected every so many years.

Muhammad's choice to move to Medina, a city some 300 kilometres to the north of Mecca and known then as Yathrib, was spurred by an invitation from the civic leaders, some of whom had already converted to his ideals. Muhammad had already approached civic leaders in the town of Ta'if some 90 kilometres south-east of Mecca but they had flatly rejected his overtures and he was vilified in the streets. The authorities in Yathrib, however, concerned about the effects of tribal feuding in the area, needed the help of a pragmatic and morally sound arbitrator from outside. For this they turned to Muhammad, offering him a secure base in return. He dispatched some 60 sympathetic families to Yathrib in small inconspicuous groups, after which he and his remaining followers escaped Mecca. They fled first to a cave in the mountains south of Mecca where they stayed for three days before turning northwards to reach their safe haven after a journey of some five more days.

Events of a more mystical nature, recorded in the Qur'anic surah named Al Isra, suggest that in 621 CE, shortly after the rejection of his overtures to the townspeople of Ta'if, the Prophet was transported to Jerusalem in a fragment of time during the night and from there he ascended to visit Paradise. Some Muslim commentators interpret this incident as a visionary experience while others give it

Below and opposite:
The Ascension of the prophet
Muhammad from a 16th-
century Persian manuscript.

more literal credence. The angel Jibril carried Muhammad from Mecca to the al-Aqsa mosque (see p. 71) where he met previous prophets including Abraham, Moses, Jesus and others. He was taken up to the heavens to witness the signs of God and it was on this journey that the five daily prayers were prescribed (see p. 103). He was then taken back to the Ka'aba, the whole experience lasting a few hours of a night.

The move to Yathrib marked a turning point in Muhammad's life. While the Meccan authorities rattled sabres and demanded his capture and return, the people of Yathrib by and large accepted his beliefs and ministry, though a "fifth column" of Meccan and Jewish subversives known as the Hypocrites, intent on undermining Muslim interest, was operating inside the city. Despite such local irritations, within a remarkably short space of time Muhammad was, in effect, the governing authority. He surrounded himself with clan supporters and others known as *ansari* or "helpers" drawn from local farming stock, established a Bill of Rights for all ethnic groups in the place that became renamed Medinat-un-Nabawi (literally, "the city of the Prophet"). Later the title was contracted to Medina, the City, which declared its independence as an autonomous state. Muhammad was given sweeping powers to carry through his long-desired programme of social reform and to promote the new Muslim ideology and the ritual practices of what was now recognized as Islam.

Converts to the new faith were expected to take an oath of allegiance, which became known as the "First Pledge of 'Aqaba", called after the place at Mecca to which pilgrimages were made. It included the following terms.

> *We shall not associate anyone with Allah, whether in worship, attributes, power or*
>   *authority.*
> *We shall not commit adultery, fornication, neither practice or spread any other indecency.*
> *We shall not steal or take the property of another in any manner or under any pretence.*
> *We shall not practice the custom of killing children.*
> *We shall not falsely accuse or slander anyone.*
> *We shall not disobey you in good deeds and just cause.*
> *We shall always follow you, be it hard or easy, to our liking or not, and we shall act*
>   *according to your commands.*
> *We shall follow and obey your decisions even if it is to our disadvantage in favour of others.*
> *We shall not oppose those persons who are deserving of authority or position.*
> *We shall uphold truth and justice and stand firm under all circumstances.*
> *In matters of our (Muslim) religion, we shall not bring the name of Islam into disrepute,*
>   *disgrace, or blame.*

To a large extent the move to Medina also turned Muhammad from private person to public figure and the change is reflected in the differing emphases of the Meccan and Medinan *surahs* of the Qur'an. The former focus largely on doctrinal matters and Muhammad's personal view of ethics, while the latter are more concerned with laying down a political and legal framework for the expanding Muslim community in western Arabia.

Militant opposition from Mecca proved an ongoing problem for the security of the Muslims and the need to respond was heightened when, between 624 and 627 CE, the Meccan forces, supported by Jewish factions and other Arabian tribes, mounted several abortive attacks on the defenders of Medina, most notable of which were the pitched battles of Uhud and Badr. The Muslims were able to claim victory despite their numbers being smaller and suffering notable losses. It is suggested though that it was the rising tide of widows and orphans that prompted Muhammad to take several more wives under his protection between his 56th and 60th year. These widows included Umm Salamah whose husband had been killed in 625 at the Battle of Uhud and Umm Habiba. Two of the other woman that he married are known by names Juwayriah and Safiyah and were apparently prisoners of war who subsequently adopted the Muslim faith. Muhammad then received a revelation that limited the permissible number of wives to four and, although he did not abandon any of his family, he entered no further marriage contracts during the remaining years of his life.

The last of the battles for control of Medina took place in 627 CE, known as the Battle of the Allies and by 628 Muhammad and Abu Bakr were assembling a much-strengthened Muslim force of some 10,000 fighting men made up of Medinan Arabs

and nomadic Bedouins. The military build-up had been gradual over a period of time during which the subversive elements in Medina were whittled down and the Muslim position was consolidated. After the death of the Sassanid King Chosroes II in 628, Muhammad was aided to no small extent by the conversion to Islam of Badhan, the Abyssinian governor of southern Arabia.

Muhammad's initial strategy was to weaken the Meccan economy by mounting hit-and-run raids on caravans operating between Mecca and Syria in order to destabilize commerce. These followed a form of limited military operation familiar in Arab tribal conflict and known as the *ghazwa*. It relied on the effective use of swords and spears, bows and arrows being the favoured weapons of the Bedouins, and was aimed at both destroying the enemy's manpower and taking its wealth as booty.

Matters approached a critical point when the Prophet and 1500 of his companions left for Mecca to perform the annual pilgrimage in 628. Their path was blocked at a place called Hudaybiyah and fraught negotiations produced only a compromise agreement that they could make the *hajj* on the following year. Towards the end of 629, however, the Quraysh leaders reneged on the agreement by aiding a punitive assault on the tribe of one of Muhammad's supporters, Bani Khuza'ah. By 630 the forces under Muhammad were set to advance from their stronghold in Medina. They attacked the Meccans and besieged the city for a period before its inhabitants were persuaded to surrender without bloodshed. They had been informed that if they remained in their houses or took refuge in the Ka'aba they would not be harmed. Muslim forces also triumphed against the well-fortified town of Ta'if whose inhabitants eventually agreed to peaceful surrender. In a final reprisal against opponents in Medina, mainly seen as Jews and Hyprocrites, Muhammad was not so benevolent. He ordered a massacre of men remaining after others had been forcibly exiled.

Having accepted the voluntary submission of Mecca, Muhammad, the Holy Prophet, had been hailed as the supreme popular authority in the Arabian peninsula and the various tribal delegations that converged on the city were now willing to accept conversion from their old local religions to Islam. The focus of Muhammad's attention moved to issues closer to his heart, those of religion. In the centre of Mecca stood a sanctuary, known on account of its shape as the Ka'aba or "cube". Time-honoured tradition maintained that the original building had been constructed by the Hebrew patriarch, Ibrahim, who had dedicated it as a shrine to the universal God of the Old Testament, El. Later it had been taken over by pre-Islamic Arab tribes and used as a pagan temple, dedicated to deities of the traditional fertility-orientated religion of the ancient Near East. Muhammad felt it appropriate to restore this place of ancient worship, built by a prophet with whom he identified as one of his predecessors, in honour of a God in whom he also placed his faith. According to the Qur'an, the Ka'aba held a unique position for him.

Follow the faith of Ibrahim. He was an upright man, not an idolator.

The first temple to be built for mankind was that at Bakkah (Mecca),

A blessed site, a beacon for the nations.

In it there are veritable signs and the place where Ibrahim stood.

Whosoever enters it is safe.

Pilgrimage to the house is a duty to God for all who can make the journey.

(Qur'an: 3. 96)

Above and left: *The prophet Muhammad rides at the head of his followers en route to the Battle of Badr where he confronted and overwhelmed hostile Meccan forces. Detail from Turkish manuscript of 1368.*

Muhammad had the Ka'aba stripped of its idolatrous trappings and announced it as the most sacred shrine of Islam to which future generations of the faithful would make their pilgrimage or *hajj*. He also offered the Jewish and Christian minorities a degree of self-government on account of the similarities of the revelations that their faiths shared with Islam and he referred to them as "the People of the Book".

One immediate consequence of this change of political and cultural identity in Arabia was that the hostility of the dominant powers in the Middle East, the Byzantines and the Persians, was aroused and threats to attack Medina from the north ensued. In 630 Muhammad instructed his army under the command of his general, Usama, to take a military campaign to Syria and to post a permanent military presence on the northern borders of Arabia. The Syrian expedition lasted for two years and all of the subsequent major battles that took place during Muhammad's declining years were fought on the northern Arabian front using volunteer troops.

In 631, having established his home in Medina, the Prophet returned to Mecca for what transpired to be his last pilgrimage since he was already ill with a fever. Many of the Meccans now embraced Islam and he was accompanied on the

Right: The prophet Muhammad delivers the final sermon of his life in the mosque in Mecca before returning to Medina where he died in 632 CE.

hajj, it is said, by 120,000 fellow pilgrims. In Mecca he delivered a memorable sermon in which he provided an overview of his social reforms and stressed the great unity of Muslims. He confirmed all humankind descended from Adam and Eve and that no Arab could therefore claim superiority over a non-Arab and vice versa. He reminded his followers to observe the Islamic religious calendar and that women had earned new rights of respect under the Islamic code, while old rights in respect of such crimes as homicide were waived. He was, he told his congregation, leaving to posterity his Qur'an (the Word) and his sunnah (the way), which, if both were followed diligently, would never lead people astray. He made the final, pointed observation that no other prophet or apostle would bring divine revelation in his wake and that he had delivered the ultimate message of Allah to God's people. On this basis later religious leaders in Islam such as Baha'ullah, the spiritual leader of the Baha'is, and Mirza Ghulam Ahmad, the founder of the Ahmadis, whose claims appear to place them with the prophets, have been considered akin to heretics by the mainstream Sunnis.

Tradition has it that during the return trip to Medina, the rapidly weakening Muhammad stopped at a place called Qadir Khum and presented his adopted son-in-law and cousin, 'Ali ibn Abi Talib, to those accompanying him with words that seemed to imply 'Ali to be his successor.

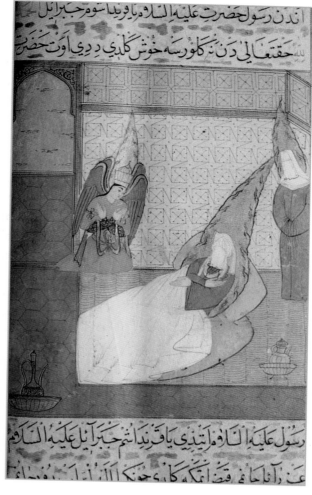

His words, "Everyone whose patron I am, also has 'Ali as their patron" regrettably were destined to trigger the first accountable split in the unity of Islam. The Prophet died in Medina with his wife 'A'isha by his side and was laid to rest there, aged 63, on June 8, 632, two years before his trusted supporter and comrade-in-arms, Abu Bakr, also died having been appointed as the first khalifa.

These are the traditions of the Prophet's life in which all Muslims firmly believe. It had been one of unremitting austerity where personal possessions, even at the height of his authority, consisted of prayer mats, blankets, jugs and other simple requirements. Material inheritance at his death amounted to a white mule, some ammunition and a piece of property that he had gifted away during his life. Among his last words were that, "the community of Prophets is not one of inheritance. Whatever we leave is for charity." In his lifetime Muhammad had brought a new and monotheistic religion to the peoples of western Arabia, improved their lives immeasurably, given them statehood with a well-organized and well-armed infrastructure and dispensed an indelible brand of faith and inspiration to the growing Muslim world.

Above: A Turkish medieval painter depicts the angel of death requesting the life of the prophet Muhammad on his deathbed in Medina. His daughter Fatima looks on.

3 THE EARLY YEARS

ISLAM DID NOT BEGIN ITS REAL CONSOLIDATION UNTIL AFTER THE death of the Prophet. In the thirty years after Muhammad's death in 632 CE the earliest successors to the leadership of Islam included four *khalifas* or caliphs elected by the elder statesmen of the new movement. In the eyes of Sunnis these patriarchs, Abu Bakr, 'Umar, 'Uthman and 'Ali are the Al-*Khulafa-ur-Rashidun*, the "four rightly guided caliphs", although the authority of the first three is strongly disputed by the Shi'is. As is true in the origins of most religious movements the record of this period is characterized by a central core of historical fact, which may have been embellished by authors and religious leaders. In the early years little was committed to paper and the account was largely passed from person to person as an oral tradition with inevitable adornments and inconsistencies being incorporated along the way.

It also has to be said at the outset of this chapter that one of the fundamentals that distinguishes early Islam from Christianity, at least in practice, rests in its all-embracing status. Islam is not something to be found within the community, it *is* the community. One of the more memorable utterances credited to Jesus during his ministry is that recorded in Mark's Gospel and paraphrased in Matthew when he responded to questions put to him by the Pharisees in Jerusalem concerning the paying of tribute money. In his reply he effectively set the seal on a separation between affairs of State and Church by saying, "Render to Caesar the things that are Caesar's, and to God the things that are God's" (Mark 12. 17). In the course of the first three centuries of Christendom this advice was followed and the machinery became established within the Roman Catholic and Apostolic Church that effectively distanced its control from that of secular government. The ecclesiastical organization included separate laws and a separate hierarchy and it was only after the conversion of the Emperor Constantine and the subsequent endorsement of Christianity as the official religion of the Empire that Church and State drew closer and became somewhat uneasy bedfellows.

Islam was never presented in this way, either by Muhammad or any of those who came in his wake. Muhammad became a sovereign leader of the first Muslim state during his lifetime, something that among the first-century Jews may have been hoped for in Jesus Christ (*messiah* is a term that gives a sense both of the "anointed one" and "the deliverer") but was never realized. The message of Muhammad included the idea that he was delivering not only a culmination of all that had gone before but also inaugurating a new beginning and a new state. It was a society where words like "religious" and "secular" became meaningless and in fact they do not exist in classical Arabic. The name "Muslim" implies total surrender to Allah and since humanity was seen to be wholly answerable to the one divine force in its affairs, both in and out of the mosque, Islam was not just a religious community but a political force set to function at all levels of society and in all its activities. This distinction marking it out from Christianity has never been lost.

As with many spiritual innovators of the past, during his lifetime Muhammad was the political focus of his movement but it was not among his foremost objectives to form a body politic. He was interested primarily in delivering the message that he had received from God. Following his death there was no successor in the matter of prophethood because he was deemed to be the last of the prophets and therefore no future prophet could stand in his stead. That he regarded himself as an ordinary human being without any claim to divinity comparable to that of Jesus Christ is made abundantly clear in the Qur'an.

> *Muhammad is no more than an apostle:*
> *Other apostles have passed away before him.*
> *If he die or be slain, will you recant?*
>
> (Qur'an: 3. 144)

Being an apostle of Allah, however, had not been Muhammad's only role, whether he wished it or not. He had also become the leader of the embryo Muslim state and in this

Right: *The Prophet Muhammad seated amidst other holy men, from an early 14th-century manuscript compiled during the Mongol era.*

context there was an urgent a need to appoint a head of the *ummah*, the name given to Islamic community in Arabia. Words like "ruler" and "sovereign" are applied loosely since in the eyes of a devout Muslim his sovereign is Allah and the *khalifa* is only worthy of the name if he is also a servant of God. This ideal may have been true in the days of the patriarchs but over the course of time, as we shall discover, the caliphate became virtually indistinguishable from a position of sovereignty. Ostensibly Muhammad was interested only in communicating the word of God and inviting submission to the will of Allah. Nonetheless it would be naïve to assume that he did not see himself partly in the mould of a political reformer championing the cause of the ordinary Arab in a world of considerable social inequality. It explains much of why the affluent merchants of Mecca had set their faces against him.

As the successor to the Prophet, the first *khalifa* was required to ensure that the path laid down by Muhammad was continued. The religion was considered to have been delivered in a state of perfection and therefore the responsibility of the caliphate was to ensure that all laws were made strictly in accordance with the Qur'an and the *sunnah*. This immediately opened the way for the beginnings of dissent between the Meccan followers who had moved with Muhammad to Medina and the Medinans themselves. These two factions were known at first as the *muhajirun* (emigrants) and *ansar* (helpers). The dispute revolved around whether the new leader should be 'Ali ibn Abi Talib, the adopted son, who according to a popular tradition Muhammad had appointed during his last journey to Medina, or whether the faithful lieutenant and friend, Abu Bakr, should be elected as *khalifa*, since conflicting opinion felt that it was he who had been appointed by the Prophet and he who had been the first adult male to convert to Islam.

Above: *A surah of the Holy Qur'an is revealed to the Prophet Muhammad during a battle.*

ABU BAKR

Tradition maintains that, although Abu Bakr was not present at the death of Muhammad, he was the first to whom 'A'isha turned and it was he who broke the news to the Muslim community in Medina. The majority of the activists among early followers considered that Muhammad had identified Abu Bakr as the rightful heir to the leadership and so in 632 they elected him as the first *khalifa*, a term through which they exercised a degree of diplomacy since it implied not only a successor but also a second-in-command. One might wonder at this choice when Muhammad had allegedly presented his adopted son-in-law and cousin, 'Ali, to those accompanying him on his last journey with the words, "Everyone whose patron I am, also has 'Ali as their patron." In a society used to polygamy, however, no particular significance could be attached to 'Ali's marriage to the Prophet's surviving child, Fatima, although his elevated position as

Above: *The Prophet Muhammad pledges the hand of his daughter Fatima in marriage to her cousin 'Ali. 18th-century painting.*

Muhammad's adopted son would have carried more significance for those who supported him as the rightful successor.

To understand the level of resistance to 'Ali taking on the leadership of Islam requires a brief glimpse of the way in which dynasties were regarded in the ancient world of the Middle East. For civilizations like those of the Persians, and the Babylonians and Assyrians before them, kings were believed, in all intent and purpose, to be gods or at least rulers by divine right, and they ascended their respective thrones by a hereditary succession that was rarely questioned. The Israelite tribes in Palestine were no exception, acknowledging the royal House of David to be the legitimate and divinely ordered claimant to the rule of Judah. Royal fathers in other words handed down sovereignty to royal sons.

In past times the clans of Arabia had tended to accept similar dynastic traditions appointing hereditary lines of kings but, as had happened elsewhere, the practice encouraged despotism and as a result many rank-and-file Arabs had become less than enthusiastic about the value of monarchies. At the time of Muhammad's death there was also a growing mood of social dissent towards the Meccan aristocracy that ordinary people regarded as being hand-in-glove with the monarchy. A significant majority of political activists among the Muslim community came to the view that they should abandon the practice of electing leaders on the basis of hereditary succession and replace it with one whereby heads of state were chosen for their personal qualities of leadership and their ability to engender loyalty amongst their subjects.

Claims have been made that Abu Bakr was not the given name of Muhammad's successor but that he acquired it as a "tag" – it means "owner of camels" – because of his interest in camel breeding. A Meccan merchant of fairly affluent means, he was apparently known previously as Abdul Ka'aba but at times Muhammad referred to him both as Abu Bakr and as 'Atiq ibn Abi Quhafa. He had been the first convert to Muhammad's beliefs outside of the Prophet's own family and was of similar age to him or a little younger. When the Prophet became increasingly infirm it was Abu Bakr who led the faithful in prayer. It seems that, from time to time, he visited the cave that Muhammad used as his contemplative retreat and he accompanied Muhammad on the *hegira* or escape from Mecca to Medina. His daughter 'A'isha had become the favourite wife of Muhammad in his later life and it was she who was at his bedside when he died. Among the descriptions of the first *khalifa* is one that 'A'isha allegedly drew herself, although it may be said to present a less than attractive profile. "He was a man with fair skin, thin, emaciated, with a sparse beard, a slightly hunched frame, sunken eyes and protruding forehead."

It has been said that the Prophet conferred on Abu Bakr the epithet *al-Siddiq*, meaning "one who always speaks the truth" and some traditions maintain that he was a pious man without any particularly aggressive traits while others place him in history as a military genius. The latter claim may be the more accurate because it was under his caliphate that opposition to Islam was forcibly eliminated in Arabia, although the triumph was not without its setbacks. A number of the tribes rebelled against Abu Bakr's leadership and there were even claims of other prophets arising including al-Aswsad al-'nsi, Tulayha al-Asadi and Musaylima. Various internal revolts had to be put down in a fraught period between 632 and 633 that became known in some quarters as the "Wars of Apostasy", *al-Ridda*. A number of false prophets came and went during these uprisings and it is on record that Musaylima was slain in a skirmish known as the Battle of al-Yamama. Some of the dissent concerned such material issues as the handing over of *zakah* or alms, which Abu Bakr's opponents considered had been due to Muhammad alone and should be abandoned. Abu Bakr also launched the first assault on lands beyond Arabia largely under the leadership of a favoured general, Khalid bin Walid, whose military genius was widely recognized. Arguably Abu Bakr set in motion the process of empire-building, although the official justification was that the Byzantines and others constituted a threat to Muslim sovereignty. He ordered attacks on Syria and Iraq and, had he not died first, would have opened a second front against the Sassanids in Persia.

There exists a popular belief that Abu Bakr began the process of collecting together the material of the Qur'an and that he handed to Usama, the old general who had first commanded the military machine during the lifetime of Muhammad, a code of conduct: "Do not desert your posts or your comrades and do not be found guilty of disobedience. Do not kill old men, women or children and do not damage date palms nor cut down fruit trees. Do not slaughter sheep, cows or camels unless to provide food. Do not molest holy men who live in monasteries but leave them in seclusion."

'UMAR

When Abu Bakr died two years after his leader at the age of 63, he recommended not 'Ali but 'Umar bin Al-Khattab to become the second *khalifa* and persuaded the military to give their backing. It was 'Umar who effectively pursued the expansion of Muslim-held territory begun by Abu Bakr. During the following decade he recruited many of the Bedouin tribesmen in the north and his combined ranks overthrew the regimes in Damascus, Jerusalem, Alexandria, Persia and Libya by force of arms. Little is known of his biography that can be verified with any degree of historical certainty and it is clear that the account which has come down to us has since been adorned with a certain amount of mythology. He was a father-in-law of Muhammad and tradition has it that he had at first opposed the new Islamic ideology but was converted to Islam when he overheard recitation of part of the Qur'an at the home of his sister. He adopted an ascetic lifestyle, wore the clothes

Above: *Illustrated page from a copy of the Holy Qur'an depicting Islamic forces engaged in a cavalry battle.*

of a penitent and became a strict disciplinarian, beating those who broke the law with a whip that he carried as a trademark of his office.

During the lifetime of Muhammad, 'Umar was involved in much of the early military campaigning and it was he who had backed Abu Bakr to take the first caliphate. Historical records show that it was under his suzerainty that Muslim expansion beyond the borders of Arabia truly gained pace. The Sassanid army was defeated in 636 in a decisive pitched battle at Qadisiyya and its seriously weakened ranks were forced to retreat, first from northern Iraq which fell to the Muslims and then into the western part of Persia. In 642 'Umar's troops again confronted the Persians near a town called Nihavand and comprehensively routed them. Terminally weakened, the Sassanids capitulated and the last of their rulers Yazdegird, fled to Khurasan to the south-east of the Caspian Sea where he was killed in 651 or 652. When the Muslim armies overran the Persian heartland they began a policy of repression against Zoroastrian followers and any that were unwilling to convert to Islam were forced to retreat into remote areas where they clung to a poverty-stricken existence.

On the Syrian front further to the west, the Byzantine armies were faring little better. In 635 'Umar attacked Damascus. The first assault failed and he was obliged to retreat to the town of Yarmuk where he again met the Byzantines and this time defeated them. The following year the Byzantine commander, Artabun, is said to have assembled a sizeable force at Ajnadin in Palestine where another significant battle was fought and the Byzantines were again defeated with heavy losses. Their remnants retreated to Jerusalem to regroup and the Muslim army marched on various key defensive positions including the towns of Nablus, Sabtah and Gaza. This effectively opened a route of advance towards a by now heavily defended Jerusalem. The city was put under siege during the winter of 636 and the position of the attacking forces under Amr bin al-As became strengthened by the arrival of contingents from the north where the commanding Muslim general, Abu Ubaida, had already secured a comprehensive victory.

Finding himself in an increasingly untenable position militarily, the Byzantine Patriarch of Jerusalem sued for peace on the condition that 'Umar received his surrender in person. 'Umar received conflicting advice from the man who was to be his successor, 'Uthman, and from 'Ali. It was the view of 'Uthman that 'Umar's personal presence at the surrender of Jerusalem would amount to a meaningless gesture. 'Ali argued that, since Jerusalem was sacred not only to Jews and Christians but to Muslims, 'Umar should accept the surrender. Popular tradition suggests that 'Umar travelled from Medina and met the Muslim army commander in the town of Jabia, walking on foot and accompanied by one servant who rode a camel. He is then claimed to have approached Jerusalem without military escort. The whole episode, however, has been somewhat glamorized over the years it seems likely that, in reality, a Muslim army guard accompanied him. After receiving the keys of the city, he apparently ordered the protection of Christian sites. Another tradition indicates that, as one of his instructions before leaving Jerusalem and returning to office in Medina, he ordered the building of a mosque that was to carry his name.

The military expansion was apparently unstoppable. In the north the Muslims consolidated their hold over Iraq and Armenia and on the southern front they marched into Byzantine-controlled Egypt which was handed over to 'Umar in a peace treaty of 641, three years before his death. The success of the Muslim forces was attributable in part to their high degree of mobility. Often history records them advancing over substantial distances to take strategic objectives while going around

Left: *Shi'a soldiers having fallen as martyrs of their faith during an early conflict.*

areas of potential resistance along the way. They relied on rapid hit-and-run sorties using lightly equipped camels and horses and could readily out-manoeuvre the more heavily armed Byzantine and Persian troops that were accompanied by cumbersome baggage trains. The Muslim soldier did not need long supply lines. He was used to frugal living and a high degree of self-reliance, taking what he needed for sustenance, by fair means or foul, from the countryside through which he passed. Only when they had secured the key positions would the Muslim forces return to "mop up" armed remnants in the regions through which they had passed. In many instances little or no resistance was put up at this late stage in a campaign.

During his time in the caliphate 'Umar was undoubtedly heavy-handed in wielding his authority but he also appears to have exercised a degree of both pragmatism and wisdom in civilian matters. He established a unique religious register called the diwan, made of close followers of Muhammad and other intellectuals who would study the doctrine and ethics of Islam for the benefit of the community, in

Below: The Prophet Muhammad's flight to exile in Medina from Mecca in September 622 CE became known as the hegira.

return for which they would receive state support. 'Umar recognized clearly that the Muslim Empire, expanding through the regions of the Middle East with breathtaking speed, needed an efficient political infrastructure if it was not to collapse on itself. His pragmatism showed in a reluctance to centralize government or to insist on the forcible conversion of populations in conquered lands to Islam, both moves that might have alienated local support. Lands that had been abandoned by movement of refugees were effectively confiscated but otherwise vassal states were to a large extent free to pursue their own faiths, languages and customs, and to maintain a degree of autonomy under the jurisdiction of an Islamic governor or *emir*. They were given the status of *dhimmi* or "protected peoples". 'Umar is also credited with having established the system of Islamic dating, whereby the year 622 CE, that of the *hegira* or flight from Mecca to Medina became 1 AH.

'Umar set up the first public treasury and established a comparatively sophisticated fiscal system throughout the Muslim-controlled territories. He realized that efficient funding of the empire was vital and introduced a special form of taxation in the occupied lands known as *jizya*, to be supervised by local financial officers called 'emils. The army was also brought under direct control by the state. Muslim forces were housed in garrison cities and their troops were funded with cash wages paid out by specially appointed pursers or *'arifs*. The military garrison towns known as *amsars* became fundamental to Muslim strategy for controlling the expanding empire. Some were founded within existing centres of population like Damascus but others were developed specifically for the purpose and were often sited in places where they could quickly accommodate Bedouins brought in from the desert areas. In time a number of the *amsars* became recognizable names on the map and functioned in their own right as urban centres, including Basra in Iraq, and Fustat (modern Cairo) in Egypt. Others such as Kufa in Iraq declined but in its hey-day it housed a force of some 40,000 and served as the launch pad for the Muslim invasion of the Caucasus. During the early course of invasion and conquest the Muslim armies swelled their coffers with substantial amounts of booty and also acquired substantial numbers of slaves who were put to use in domestic duties rather than military support.

'UTHMAN

'Umar died in 644 CE, said to have been slain by a slave carrying a personal grudge, and he was succeeded by 'Uthman ibn Affan as the third *khalifa*. 'Uthman was of a different calibre to 'Umar and in many ways he conformed to the image of the aristocratic dynastic rulers of the tribes whose social injustices in Mecca had offended Muhammad. 'Uthman's predecessors, Abu Bakr and 'Umar, had emerged from the middle ranks of the Quraysh tribe in Mecca and had been elected with popular support. 'Uthman, by contrast, was a highly placed member of the aristocratic Umayyad tribe whose influence in pre-Islamic Mecca had been substantial and had been opposed to the ideology being promoted by Muhammad. A committee of six Meccans belonging to the Quraysh decided his election in an atmosphere of dispute

Below: *Mosaics depicting fantasy towns, landscapes and trees on the outer facade of the Prayer Hall at the Umayyad Mosque, Damascus.*

over the role of 'Ali that refused to go away. Significantly, perhaps, the committee did not include any representatives of the Medinan clans who sympathies lay with 'Ali but involved 'Ali himself. The committee was faced with two choices, the son-in-law and devout apostle of Muhammad, still waiting in the wings for his moment to shine, or 'Uthman who had already acquired a formidable reputation as a politician and military strategist. For the selection committee, faced with managing the complexities of empire, it was the practical qualities of leadership presented by 'Uthman that took precedence over the spiritual convictions of 'Ali. 'Uthman also appears to have been willing to continue the expansionist policies put in place by 'Umar.

'Uthman's succession proved more controversial, however, since it also opened the way for the Meccan upper classes to restore some of their lost prestige. Although he ruled for some 12 years, 'Uthman may never have enjoyed wide backing outside his own social circle and detractors were quick to accuse him of nepotism. He appointed Umayyads to key positions in government at home and abroad and these favoured men included Mu'awiya who was destined to become the fifth *khalifa*. Mu'awiya was handed the favoured post of governor over Syria and northern Iraq. In terms of military achievements 'Uthman led the successful Muslim conquest of Libya in North Africa and oversaw the consolidation of Islamic dominance in the remaining Persian territories formerly controlled by the Sassanids. Some of this process of expansion was carried out as the consequence of a growing need to generate more state revenue through taxation of foreigners.

While enjoying a level of military achievement, 'Uthman is said to have failed in a number of civil matters: for example, there was a decline in the effective financial management of the empire. He had added substantially to the number of individuals being paid through the diwan on the "civil list" and this put pressure on the wages that were available for the troops. Toward the end of his caliphate he was obliged to put a hold on military expansion and the ensuing peace allowed the various tribal factions time to consider what they perceived as injustices on the home front. In a mood of rising civil discontent, riots broke out in Medina in 656 during which 'Uthman was assassinated, with the finger of blame pointed conveniently at Khariji separatists who were becoming increasingly anarchic and moving toward rejection of any authority. They had already adopted the view that anyone could take the role of leader providing that he had earned the grass-roots support of the Muslim brotherhood and 'Uthman did not exactly fit the image of popular leadership. Nonetheless, there is no hard evidence of Khariji involvement and members of any number of disaffected clans may have carried out the assassination. Other reports indicate that he was murdered by discontented Egyptians.

'Uthman's reign may have been marked by armed conquest and degrees of civil unrest, yet there were more creditworthy sides to his term of office. He brought a degree of scholarship into government and tradition claims that he was the *khalifa* who first authorized the copying of a definitive text of the Qur'an. Prior to this the *surahs* had largely been circulated by word of mouth, but the ranks of those who possessed the ability to remember and recite the verses were becoming thinned and there was an increasing risk of elements being forgotten or distorted. The authorization was not, however, without its critics since it is claimed that 'Uthman had any unauthorized copies of the Qur'an that were already in circulation burnt. Some scholars of Islam have now put forward controversial evidence that this may indeed have happened and that the version of the Qur'an handed down to posterity may not be the only one to have appeared (see p. 91), though purists deny this possibility.

'ALI

The violent death of 'Uthman was to precipitate the first of a series of devastating civil wars between those for and against what amounted to the "rule of kings". His assassination marked the first occasion on which Muslim had openly fought and slain Muslim. There remained a majority, essentially Meccans, who considered that Abu Bakr and the *khalifas* (though not necessarily Umayyad caliphs) were the legitimate heirs of Muhammad, but opposing them was a smaller faction that considered the only acceptable "succession" to be through 'Ali and his descendants since they amounted to Muhammad's family. The former lobby became known as Sunnis or *al-sunnah wa-l-jamaa*, so-called because they claimed to be the followers of *sunnah*, the traditions of the Prophet. The latter became Shi'is or *shi'at Ali*, meaning the "followers of 'Ali". The Kharijis broke away as separatists in 658 CE, adding to the atmosphere of strife, and their influence steadily waned, although prior to this time they seem to have been more involved in establishing law and influencing policy. They supported the Shi'a view that 'Ali ibn Abi Talib was better placed as leader of Islam.

'Ali was effectively launched into office as the fourth *khalifa* by Medinans disenchanted after more than 20 years of Meccan domination that was seen by detractors to include nepotism, favouritism, misadministration and unwanted religious innovation. Yet 'Ali proved no more popular than his predecessor. It was his appointment that led to the first civil war between the Umayyads and the Shia supporters of 'Ali. An atmosphere already charged with considerable unrest and grumbling among the Meccans fomented to open hostility when 'Ali proved reluctant to bring the killers of 'Uthman to justice. Two of the Meccan leaders who had been former 'Ali supporters drummed up passions for a rebellion but this initial offensive was crushed during the Battle of the Camel fought out near the southern port of Basra. The event was so named because it is said to have been observed by A'isha, Muhammad's widow, from a vantage point seated in a palanquin on the back of a camel. She had been deeply opposed to 'Ali's failure to bring the assassins of 'Uthman to justice and effectively rallied the armed revolt against him.

'Ali's problems had only just begun. In the north Mu'awiya, the Umayyad governor of Syria and Iraq who had been appointed by 'Uthman, withdrew all support from 'Ali and in the spring of 657 the two opposing sides clashed violently at a place called Siffin. One of the consequences of this inconclusive military action,

which was to result in a truce based on arbitration, was to lose 'Ali a degree of popular support. A number of his troops deserted, fleeing to Nahrawan on the slopes to the east of the River Tigris where they established a predominantly Khariji settlement. The Syrians recognized that the balance of Muslim power was poised to shift and prudently they pledged allegiance to Mu'awiya as the legitimate *khalifa*. Mu'awiya then used his strengthened position to usurp 'Ali and to take control of Egypt in the autumn of 657.

The extent of 'Ali's authority was thus substantially weakened and he became ruler of little more than central and southern Iraq among the occupied territories. One of his last military successes was mounted against the renegade forces in Nahrawan but he himself was to be slain by a Khariji assassin in 661. The killing was seen to be a consequence of the ongoing conflict between squabbling factions, and 'Ali's death effectively closed the door on a caliphate elected by the people. The old policy of a meritocracy and rule through local administration was to be replaced with a form of centralized authority that amounted to little more than dynastic dictatorship.

Predictably it was to the Umayyad supreme commander, Mu'awiya, that the fifth caliphate was granted. His accession did not immediately end the civil unrest but during his time of office he would effectively neutralize the remaining opposition of the minority Shi'is and Kharijis. In doing so, ironically, he was to establish precisely the kind of family-based sovereignty that had been so much resented. During the course of almost a century the Umayyads moved the administration to Damascus in Syria and made it into the capital of an Islamic world that would stretch from the western borders of China to southern France.

The centralization of authority under Mu'awiya ended what was to become seen romantically as the golden age of early Islam, the idealized period of rule and conquest under the first four *khalifas* who are viewed retrospectively as the only Islamic patriarchs to be elected "by the people, for the people" and to be faithful to the traditions laid down by Muhammad. All, in one sense or another, were related to the Prophet by marriage. The Umayyads and their *khalifas* were destined to control the growing Muslim Empire until 750 and they brought what, to modern Shi'is, has represented more than 1,000 years of illegitimate government. Traditionally Sunnis have accepted the legitimacy of the first four who they regard as the "rightly guided caliphs". Shi'is, on the other hand, reject the legitimacy of the first three and recognize only 'Ali, as Muhammad's chosen but largely thwarted successor.

Opposite: *The fourth khalifa, 'Ali ibn Abi Talib, the adopted son of the Prophet Muhammad, receiving a blow during The Battle of the Camel. From a 17th-century mural.*

Below: *Mosaic decoration on a wall of the 15th century Mazar-i-Sharif mosque in northern Afghanistan. Tradition maintains that the mosque houses the tomb of the fourth khalifa, 'Ali ibn Abi Talib.*

4 The Dynastic Empire

WHEN THE EARLY PIONEERING ORDER OF ISLAM, THE RULE OF the patriarchs that Sunnis regard as the four "Rightly Guided Caliphs", came to an end, it marked the close of the first phase in the history of the Islamic peoples. It might be compared loosely with the Old Testament era of the patriarchs and judges. From that moment in time, the rule over the Muslim peoples became dynastic, founded on family and tribal descent. It involved two major Arab dynasties, those of the Umayyads and their successors the Abassids. There followed a comparatively unstable period when clans of non-Arab stock came and went with monotonous regularity, seizing power only to be thrown out and replaced by other dominant factions. An exception came with the Turkish Seljuks who managed to control the empire through much of the eleventh and twelfth centuries. Instability returned, however, and this situation continued until the thirteenth century when the first major era of Muslim power came to an end with the Mongol invasion of 1258.

THE UMAYYADS

When Mu'awiya bin Abu Sufian assumed the caliphate in 661 CE he launched a dynasty drawn from members of the Umayyad tribe, which was to revert to the hereditary line of kingship that early followers had resented and it resulted in the rejuvenation of old factional loyalties. The Umayyads held power over the Muslim Empire in the Middle East for a hundred years, rather longer in the Iberian peninsula. While this period brought a greater sense of stability to the Muslim world than it had experienced in its formative years, it was not without strife either externally and within Islam's own realms. The Shi'a minority refused to accept the legitimacy of the caliphate and the civil war rumbled on intermittently. History suggests that the Umayyad dynasty shifted its primary focus from religious concerns to those of empire-building and Islamic traditionalists claim that in this its policies differed fundamentally from those of the first four *khalifas*.

While generally tolerant of other religious beliefs and cultural traditions, the Umayyads nevertheless adopted a general policy of changing the cultural character of towns and cities they took over. In Jerusalem, for example, Muslim architects supervised a restoration programme on the walls of the Temple Mount, originally much damaged by the Romans, and they replaced the Hulda Gates, dating from the Second Temple period, so as to provide better access in the southern wall. In 691 CE, under the caliphate of Malik, the Umayyads then built the Dome of the Rock and the Al-Aqsa Mosque on the heights of the Temple Mount (see p. 71). A group of large buildings, the ruins of which were excavated in the 1970s, were erected nearby to the south and south-west of the Mount and probably served as a substantial administrative centre for the provincial Muslim government. They included one building of palatial proportions thought to have been the residence of the *khalifa* during periodic visits to the city and to have dated from the reign of one of the later Ummayad caliphs, Walid I (705–15). The Muslim planners in Jerusalem restored running water from the main aqueduct and renewed smashed drainage channels. The Umayyads also left a number of fine desert palaces to posterity. It has been suggested that the royal court frequently adopted a nomadic lifestyle, moving at different seasons of the year in order to avoid the worst of the heat and the epidemics of plague that erupted from time to time. They established various camping grounds and eventually the more permanent residences were built on the sites of these.

One of the first significant actions made by Mu'awiya was to relocate his power base: in 661 he moved the capital of the Muslim Empire from Arabia to Damascus in Syria. He was shrewd enough to realize that continued military engagement with the Byzantine Christian forces served little purpose and he concluded a truce with the Holy Roman Empire that lasted for the duration of his reign. Posterity has accorded to Mu'awiya the image of a pragmatic leader, though this is perhaps a subjective view. It is certainly true that during his time of office he ruled the Muslim-controlled lands without further hostility breaking out and he is said to have described his policy as one of restraint and tolerance: "I apply not my sword where the lash suffices, nor the lash where my tongue is adequate. If there be so much as a single hair binding me to my fellow man, I do not allow it to break. When he pulls I give ground and if he submits I pull."

Among his contributions to Islamic culture Mu'awiya also commissioned the building of the Great Mosque in Damascus (see p. 134). He died in 680 CE, passing on the caliphate to his son Yazid.

Almost immediately, under the Yazid administration, the sixth caliphate since the death of Muhammad, the Shi'a minority rebelled again, their action reaching a bloody climax when the two sides clashed in the Battle of Karbala, an incident that was to take on legendary proportions. A small force of Shi'is led by Husayn (Hussein), one of the sons of 'Ali, confronted a much larger Sunni battalion. The Shi'is were convincingly defeated and Husayn was killed. It was this slaying that led to the tradition of the glorious martyrdom among Shi'a Muslims. Medina, seen as the seat of the rebellion, was sacked and taken under the direct control of the Umayyads. The persecution of Kharijis continued so that they were dispossessed and scattered to increasingly remote areas. This setback did not prevent the Shi'a minority from continuing to plague the Sunni caliphate. A resistance movement was formed in the Hijaz under Abdullah ibn as-Zubayr and for much of the next 70 years the rebels caused difficulties in Arabia that spread over the course of time into North Africa and the Iberian peninsula.

Notwithstanding his problems Yazid himself seems to have been a cultured man, interested in Arab history, music and poetry and a connoisseur of wine, which he

Left: *The gold roof of the Dome of the Rock gleams in the dawn sunlight above the old city of Jerusalem. The Church of the Holy Sepulchre is visible in the background.*

preferred to the more traditional drink of rose sherbet. Tradition has it that his fondness for the grape earned him the soubriquet Yazid of the Vine.

The civil conflict ended under the caliphate of Yazid's successor, Abd-al Malik ibn Marwan, who assumed power in 685 and who was descended from another branch of the Umayyad clan. While maintaining the seat of authority in Damascus he effectively reunified the empire and embarked on a new phase of military expansion. Persecution of Kharijis continued but the definition of the faith of Islam was liberalized in order to accommodate an increasing number of non-Arabs who were by now accepting conversion. It was under Abd-al Malik that a substantial campaign westwards through North Africa was begun, with, it is said, the prime objective of acquiring Berber slaves. The first major victory outside of Egypt took place with the taking of the city of Carthage in 698 and the advance eventually reached the shores of the Atlantic Ocean. The military expansion led Abd-al Malik to consider the increasing problems of communication with widely flung parts of the empire and he developed one of the world's earliest postal systems.

Away from the military front Abd-al Malik was an effective administrator who introduced a range of government offices. He earned his most significant place in Islamic civic history, however, as the *khalifa* who introduced Arabic as the language of administration in the Muslim Empire, abandoning the more traditional Greek and Pahlavi. He also introduced a Muslim coinage to replace that of the Byzantines and the old Sassanid money, which, until then, had been the only currency in circulation. Further abroad he took responsibility for improving the state of agriculture in Mesopotamia (Iraq) by dredging many of the clogged irrigation canals that had been built in the Tigris Euphrates valley by the Sumerians several thousand years earlier. He also introduced the water buffalo to the southern marshes of Iraq. He died in 705 and was succeeded by Walid I as the next *khalifa*.

Above: *Archaeologists digging in the area around the south wall of the Temple Mount in Jerusalem. The silver dome of the Al-Aqsa mosque dominates the site.*

Walid was to oversee the height of Umayyad power. Under his authority Muslim territory was expanded by force of arms north through the Caucasus into southern Russia and north-east, forming a bridgehead over the River Oxus into the region known as Transoxania, thus opening a route to the fabled central Asian cities of Bukhara and Samarkand. Eventually the empire extended as far as the borders of China. In the east his armies took Kabul in modern Afghanistan and reached the valley of the Indus, the gateway to India where a considerable exchange of cultural ideas was to develop. Once again a prime motive lay in acquisition not merely of territory but manpower in the form of slaves to underpin the machinery of the empire. Ironically some of these slaves, many of whom were seconded into the military as *mamluks*, meaning "owned" and who then converted to Islam, were to play a significant part in the future history of the empire. Particularly those of Turkish origin proved themselves excellent fighting men and came to occupy high ranks in the Islamic armies. In the Middle Ages their descendants, swelled by new ranks of Turkish forced labour, became fundamental to the military successes of the Ottomans. Walid's reign also witnessed the death of Zayd ibn Ali, the founder of the Bedouin Zayd Shia's whose descendants predominate in the modern state of Yemen.

Walid's forces attacked the Byzantine capital of Constantinople on the Bosphorus, consolidated their hold on the North African coast as far as Morocco and Algeria and from there they were poised to take the Iberian peninsula. In the summer of 710 a substantial force under the command of Tariq ibn Zayad crossed the Straits of Gibraltar with instructions from Damascus to take as much land northwards as possible. In a symbolic gesture he set fire to his ships, thus precluding retreat and within a matter of weeks the Muslim forces had attacked and occupied the Spanish cities of Cordoba and Toledo. The region was renamed *al-Andal*, from whence came the modern word Andalusia, and the rock at the western mouth of the

Opposite: *Detail of the golden dome and the ornate exterior decoration of the Dome of the Rock in Jerusalem.*

Mediterranean became known as Gibraltar, a corruption of *jabal Tariq* or "the mountain of Tariq". Soon afterwards a much larger army under the command of General Musa ibn Nusair joined the expeditionary force.

By 713 they had acquired the southern regions of France as far north as Narbonne and the port of Toulouse. These areas of South-West Europe that had previously been under the unwelcome control of the Visigoths through peace deals made by the Holy Roman Empire seem to have acquiesced more or less willingly to new and perhaps more congenial administration than they had experienced under the 'barbarians'. Nevertheless the political situation remained extremely unpredictable, with squabbling factions of Arabs, Berbers and locals raising the temperature from time to time. A more secure form of government was not to be established until 755 under the leadership of an Umayyad prince, 'Abd ar-Rahman ibn Mu'awiya, who had escaped the massacre of his clansmen in Syria, arrived in Cordoba and set up a local caliphate. Dynastic rule was then established in Cordoba, which effectively became the western capital of the Muslim Empire and the Umayyad administration was destined to survive for rather longer than its counterpart in Damascus.

Below: An ornately carved bowl from the early Umayyad period.

From this huge imperial base in Iberia the Islamic forces were poised to take on the rest of the Holy Roman Empire in Northern Europe. The triumph was not to last, however. Although they now controlled a substantial coastline in Spain and North Africa the Muslims proved inefficient in naval warfare and were no match for the Byzantine fleets, so they could only advance effectively using land-based forces. The Umayyads used what sea power they had to invade the Balearic Islands and to move up and down the coast of North Africa but for little else strategically. The advance of Umayyad forces from Spain was halted in north-west France in 732 when they were less than 250 kilometres from Paris. Even then the presence amounted to little more than raids, as distinct from a more permanent occupation.

Under the leadership of Charles Martel the Byzantine army routed the Muslims in the Battle of Poitiers and forced them to retreat. Charles Martel, born in about 689, had begun his public career inauspiciously as *major domo* of the palace of the eastern Frankish Empire, Austrasia. He was the illegitimate son of the emperor, Pepin of Herstal. Pepin's widow, Plectrude, became regent for her grandsons but Charles usurped the throne and by 719 had extended his dominion over all the Franks. Having succeeded at Poitiers, he then took back Toulouse while the Muslims retired to Spain and regrouped.

During the remaining two decades of Umayyad control few of the *khalifas* achieved notable successes. None of the trio of Malik's sons that assumed the caliphate next, Sulayman, 'Umar II and Yazid II, reigned for longer than four years apiece. Each inherited a problem of tribal politics that refused to go away and this resulted in a backlash whereby non-tribal Muslims known as *mawali* began to recruit support for an anti-Umayyad coalition. Being foreigners, the *mawalis*, literally "clients", could not join an Arab society that was still thoroughly based on kinship. They found themselves in an ambivalent position as they came under the voluntary protection of the tribes but were to all intents and purposes treated as second-class citizens. In Persia discontent against the Umayyad caliphate was mounting as early as 718 when Muhammad ibn 'Ali, a great-grandson of one of Muhammad's paternal uncles began recruiting support for an anti-Umayyad resistance determined to restore the caliphate to the Prophet's family, the descendants of the Hashim branch of the Quraysh tribe. The Shi'a and Khariji minorities also continued to make occasional attempts at rebellion and the high taxation required to finance the military campaigns led to increasing disaffection among converts.

The last of the great Umayyad *khalifas* is generally regarded as Hisham, the fourth of Abd al-Malik's sons to succeed to the caliphate. He came to power in 724 and held office for 19 years. After his death no outstanding statesmen appear to have held the office. His successor Walid II reigned for no more than a year and the last of the Umayyad *khalifas* was Marwan II who ruled the empire from 744 until 750. It was during his term that a massive earthquake struck Palestine and destroyed much of the magnificent building work that had been done by early Umayyads in Jerusalem.

Sometime before 747 the anti-Umayyad revolutionaries had established a power base in Khorasan in Persia and their subversive influence then spread to Iraq. Dissatisfied with the century of Umayyad control they had rallied behind a contender for the caliphate named Abdullah as-Saffah or Abu al-'Abbas and thus became known as the Abassids. He claimed descent from an uncle of Muhammad, al-'Abbas ibn 'Abd al-Muttalib and was not therefore of Umayyad stock. The Shi'is also backed the Abassid cause. A combination of Khorasanian muscle and Shi'a rhetoric swayed public opinion. Abdullah as-Saffah seized the Muslim caliphate in 747 or 750 (accounts are not consistent) when his forces clashed with those of Marwan at Damascus and the Umayyads were defeated in the Battle of Zab. This was a particularly bloody affair in which, except for the escape of a single aristocratic family, the entire leadership of the Umayyads was slaughtered in order to exclude the possibility of any contest over succession. The Umayyad dynasty in Spain survived for longer only because 'Abd ar-Rahman ibn Mu'awiya managed to re-establish a degree of Umayyad stability in the stronghold of Cordoba supported by other exiles including disaffected Berbers, non-Arabic Muslims or *mawalis*, Shi'is and North African Kharijis.

Below: *The cathedral mosque and Roman bridge in Cordoba, Spain.*

ABASSIDS

In Syria, in 750, Abu al-'Abbas took over the reins of power as the first *khalifa* of the new dynasty, controlling the major part of the Muslim Empire with the exception of Iberia. After four years he was succeeded by Abu Ja'far al'Mansur who ruled for the next two decades. The Abassids, representing a true branch of the Prophet's family, were destined to rule the Muslim world for more than 500 years, though, in an echo of the fate of their predecessors, their influence and power was set to wane gradually during their twilight era in the first half of the thirteenth century. By the time that they were thrown out by the Mongols in 1258 they amounted to little more than puppet figureheads and it is perhaps indicative of the instability of the dynasty that from as-Saffah's accession in 749 until the Mongol invasion, no less than 37 *khalifas* took office, some remaining there for little more than a year.

By and large the Abassids did not retain the interest of their predecessors in foreign conquest, although a year after the first Abassid caliph was sworn in, the Muslim forces routed the Chinese in the province of Transoxia and handed control to the local Samanid clan. The Muslim Empire had in other respects reached limits beyond which it could not effectively expand and so the new dynasty chose to consolidate its borders with the Christian world in the north and west, China and India in the east. Holy war or *jihad* became a thing of the past, although the principle of struggle against the infidel was still retained in Muslim tradition and in the Shari'a (see p. 175).

Lack of enthusiasm for conquest of foreign soil once more allowed attention to focus internally and, once again, it bred trouble. In the immediate aftermath of takeover the new caliphate clamped down severely on any signs of dissent amongst Shi'is and Kharijis and consolidated its hold on power with a degree of ruthlessness. In 750 one of the key political moves made by the new dynasty was to transfer the power base from Damascus in Syria to Baghdad in Iraq where the Abassids enjoyed the strongest support. The Muslim population of Syria was still home to numbers of disaffected but powerful Umayyad families. The dynastic upheaval may also have represented a cultural shift in that the Umayyads fostered an Islamic lifestyle based historically on Semitic culture whereas the Abassids placed greater store on Persian values and traditions. A more moderate argument is that the move from Damascus to Baghdad resulted in a blending of Semitic and Persian cultures. Baghdad thus earned a level of prestige reminiscent of the glory it had enjoyed during the Babylonian Empire of yesteryear. Not only was the city the new political and administrative heart of a great imperial power again, much of its ancient cultural reputation was restored.

The colours on the political map were not just changed by the emergence of a new Muslim dynasty. The year 786 saw an uprising amongst the Shi'a population in Mecca, in part a reaction to the abandoning of their principles by the Abassid caliphs. A massacre took place, after which the Shi'a survivors escaped to an area of West Africa known as the Maghrib, which today includes Morocco, Algeria, Libya and Tunisia. There they set up an independent kingdom ruled by a family known as the Idrisids. Theirs was an extreme case but, in many other places outside the Arab heartlands, men of non-Arab racial background and breeding took up the reins of authority. No longer did the caliphate in Baghdad assume absolute dominion over the empire and the administrative structure became greatly more cosmopolitan in nature, many of the provinces coming under the control of local overlords who themselves established independent dynasties. Even at their Baghdad court the Abassids were beginning to rely more on foreigners as advisers. By the turn of the ninth century a number of powerful cliques such as the Fatimids, Ayyubids and Mamluks were running what amounted to rival states in Egypt, Syria and Palestine respectively. The *mamluks* in particular were to play a significant role in the ongoing political power game. Former Turkish, Slav and Berber slaves who had been seconded into the forces at various times, often forming cavalry units, had proved themselves formidable adversaries. The overall dilution of Arab supremacy in the Muslim Empire not surprisingly caused smouldering resentment amongst conservatives. It

Below: *A fine engraving, thought to have been made in about 1600, showing the medieval city of Baghdad, Iraq.*

BAGDAD

A. der Tigerflus   C. das Landthor E. Schiffbrucke G. Moscheen oder
B. die Festung   D. Wasserthor   F. Vorstadt   Tempel

was not long before the spectre of internal strife appeared over the horizon for the fourth time in the history of the Muslim peoples.

Civil war broke out in 809 and this time it involved a power struggle, with a knock-on effect, between the sons of the fifth *khalifa* Harun ar-Rashid. The son who succeeded him was al-Amin ibn Harun, the sixth in succession, but his siblings were his rivals for the position and four years later one of them, al-Ma'mun ibn Harun, mounted a successful coup. He and a third brother, al-Mu'tasim ibn Harun, came to the timely view that, in order to safeguard against the experiences of recent years, the caliphate needed to surround itself with troops whose loyalty could be guaranteed. Arab and Persian troops largely staffed the Muslim army but their loyalty to the Abassids was coming increasingly into question. Sometime after 833, when al-Mu'tasim had gained the caliphate, he brought about a significant shift in the make-up of the military establishment by forming a fresh force whose allegiance to him was more assured. He started a programme of recruitment from among the *mamluks* and by the reign of his son, al-Wathiq, towards the mid-ninth century, these foreign soldiers had effectively displaced the Arabs and Persians in their role as defenders of the caliphate. It was not a popular move and the Abassid administration was rapidly shedding support in many Arab quarters. The move away from an Arab-dominated military exacerbated the strong resentment among many of the clans, no more so than the Khorasanian faction in Persia that had, ironically, been instrumental in giving the Abassids their power in the first place. The authority of the caliphate became eroded still further as the new army commanders assumed wider powers and eventually the office of the *khalifa* was more or less sidelined by the introduction of a new half-political, half-military institution, that of the Sultanate.

Throughout this time of internal conflict the binding sinews of the Muslim empire remained its religion, the Qur'an and the *hadith*, and the use of Arabic as a common language of communication, much as English is applied today. An exception was Persia. Its subjects had always exercised a degree of independence in their national identity and preserved their own language. Eventually in the eastern regions of the empire Persian replaced Arabic as the main language. Throughout the Muslim-held territories Islamic arts also developed their own distinctive characteristics and inspired a sense of identity among disparate groups and nationalities. The decor of the Alhambra in Spain is, for example, as recognizably Islamic as that of comparable buildings in Baghdad or Cairo. The era of control by the brothers also saw an intensified interest in all aspects of learning and, during the hey-day of the Abassids, often thought of as the golden age of the Muslim civilization, the sciences reached their greatest level of achievement.

Al-Ma'mun had been responsible for particular cultural changes during his time of office. He encouraged scholarship and was particularly instrumental in broadening Arabic culture to include the traditions of Greece and India by introducing study of Greek and Sanskrit. His successor al-Mu'tasim had already brought new concepts into Islamic ideology and theology that many conservatives viewed as tantamount

Above: An early Islamic coin minted during the Abassid dynasty.

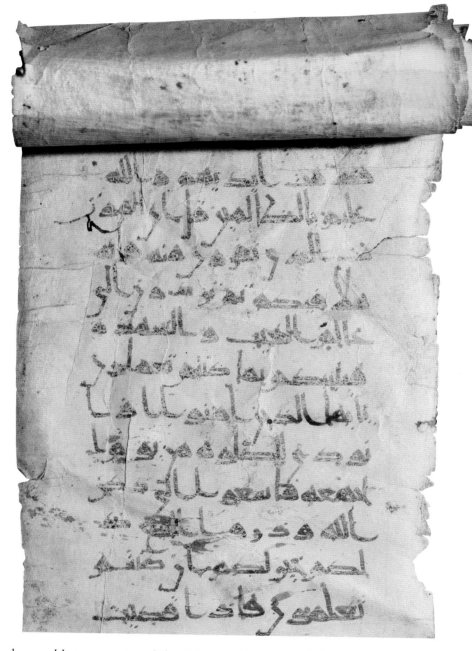

Left: *A fragment of an early copy of the Qur'an, dating from the 8th or 9th century.*

to heresy. He was convinced that Islam could learn much from Plato and other great philosophers and would gain from a broadening of rational inquiry rather than an inflexible dedication to one strand of thinking. At a more practical level, he also held to the principle that all Muslims should maintain obedience to a single ruler. He was sufficiently committed to radical change to establish a university for the promotion of his new vision, which became referred to as Mu'tasilism.

One of the most controversial aspects of Mu'tasilism was the notion that the Holy Qur'an had been created by human hand rather than being a product of divine revelation and therefore immutable. It led to the Mu'tasilite Inquisition that functioned from 833 until 848 under the authority of al-Mamun who was in sympathy with the principles set out by the school. It involved a test that the holy men of Baghdad were required to undergo, including expressing an opinion on the creation of the Qur'an. Many scholars responded with resistance, to the extent that in Damascus the *khalifa* was obliged to perform the test himself, and the innovation proved highly unpopular. The Inquisition continued into the caliphate of al-Mutawakkil (847–61) but was then dropped and any person found guilty of expressing the heresy that the Qur'an had been created by the patriarchs could have faced execution.

In about 900 one more period of expansion was to take place under the Abassid caliphate, northwards through the Caucasus and into the territory of the Volga where a sapping conflict was to continue for a hundred years against the Jewish Khazars. Eventually this resulted in Islamic power penetrating Russia.

In the Iberian peninsula the exiled Umayyads had effectively founded a rival empire, though the caliphate was not to be established there until 929. The establishment of the kingdom of Asturia by the Christian Normans effectively blocked progress northwards but meanwhile the situation in Cordoba was comparatively tranquil and Abd ar-Rahman set about an urban restoration programme. He oversaw the construction of the magnificent Emir's Palace, the *dar al-Imara*, beside the River Guadalquivir, commissioned a number of mosques and attended to the improvement of the city's defences by erecting massive boundary walls. He was never to return to Syria but he maintained a lifelong nostalgia for his homeland, expressed in his sad songs.

Below: Detail of the ornate architecture in the Cordoba mosque.

> I found a palm tree in Rusafa;
> In these western lands it is a sight so rare and I said
> "Like me you stand alone and far from home,
> You long for the children and the loved ones,
> And you have not flourished as you would in native soil.
> Like you, this is a foreign air I breathe."

As the political strength of the Abassid caliphate weakened, the *khalifas* came to occupy a position that amounted to little more than symbolic heads of state. Actual authority and military muscle passed into the hands of an assortment of powerful sultans and princes. In Baghdad the close of the ninth century saw the scholarly ranks of Sunnis who had been encouraged by al-Mu'tasim taking over more and more areas of administration at the expense of the caliphs and by the mid-tenth century the *khalifas* had lost any semblance of administrative control and could be removed and replaced at will. Actual control of the Muslim Empire in the Middle East was about to be seized by a new non-Arab dynasty from Persia.

BUYIDS AND KAKUYIDS

Two branches of a powerful family known as the Deylamids, who already controlled much of western Persia, ruled as *emirs* from about 945 until they too were overthrown in either 1055 or 1060. The Kakuyids effectively controlled the eastern part of Persia and the Buyids or Buwayhids came from the more northerly area. Named after a man called Buyeh they had begun military incursions into Abassid-controlled lands in about 930, taking the cities of Isfahan and Kerman. By 945 they were rattling the gates of Baghdad ready to take control of the empire, relegating the Sunni *khalifas* to the role of nominal figureheads. Ahmed, one of the sons of Buyeh, significantly took the title of supreme commander, the *emir al-umara*.

Late in the tenth century the Buyids expanded their area of direct control into Oman and other territories and in about 976 one of their military leaders founded a short-lived dynasty in Afghanistan called the Ghaznavids. In the east they began a holy war against the Rajputs in northern India that was to rumble on for two centuries until the Sultanate of Delhi was founded in 1206. They also, however, experienced setbacks. In North Africa in 969 the pro-Shi'a Fatimids made sweeping military gains, founding the city of Cairo as their power base and a year later a renewal of support for the Kharijis resulted in the foundation of a movement known as the Qarmatarians. Within 30 years they would form an anarchist enclave, for a short time, on the east coast of Arabia.

Among the more lasting monuments to the rule of the Buyids was the construction of the Emir's Dam across the River Kur. Muslim history, however, was destined to repeat itself. The leaders of the clans fell out with each other and gradually their hold on power declined until, after a little more than a century, they were out of office. One of the last of the emirs, Ala' al-Daula Muhammad, who held power from 1008 until 1042, made an optimistic peace deal with an aggressive faction of central Asian Turkish stock or Turkmens, known as the Seljuks. The deal would soon be broken.

SELJUKS

The Seljuks, named after a distant ancestor and stemming from a tribe known as the Ghuzz, had converted to Sunni Islam at sometime during the tenth century. Advancing from their heartland between the Caspian Sea and the River Oxus, under the command of their Sultan Togrul Beg, they took over the Persian province of Khorasan early in the eleventh century and sacked the city of Isfahan in 1051. They then forced an alliance with the local ruling clan, the Kakuyids and established control over much of central Iran. Ignoring the peace treaty they marched on Baghdad and took it from the Buyids in 1055. Ostensibly they claimed to be the guardians of the weakening caliphate, Togrul Beg naming himself diplomatically "protector of the caliph". They were, to a degree, mindful of the Fatimid dynasty of Shi'is in Egypt that had grown steadily in stature and now posed a threat to Sunni

Below: *Interest in Classical history is apparent in this 13th century Turkish Seljuk manuscript depicting the 7th-century BCE Athenian poet and statesman, Solon, engaged in discussion with his students.*

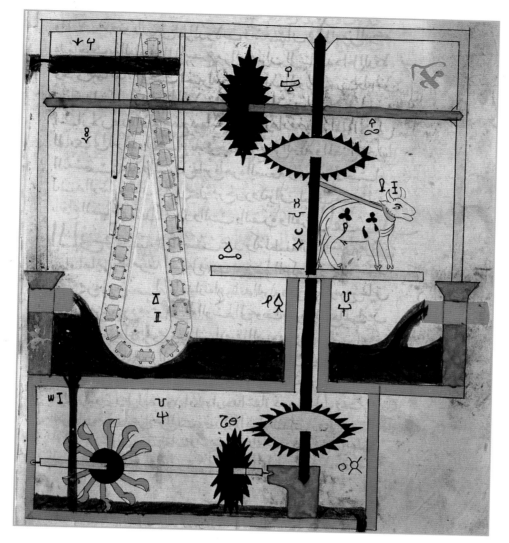

dominance of the Middle East. Nonetheless after 1055 power actually rested with the Seljuk sultanate, which did much to revive the Sunni administrative and religious institutions as well as the classical Islamic education system while also acting as a powerful buffer against the Crusaders. The dynasty was set to dominate the Muslim world of Persia, Iraq and Syria in the eleventh and twelfth centuries.

With the decline of the caliphate the Muslim Empire, constantly unstable and weakened in its authority, entered the troubled times of the Islamic Middle Ages. In November 1095, during the second year of the largely symbolic rule of *khalifa* al-Mustazhir, the Christian Pope Urban II, supported militarily by various European kings, sanctioned the First Crusade. Its stated purpose was to liberate Jerusalem and the oppressed Christian lands in the Middle East, but the underlying demand was to stem further possible Muslim advances. Although there was at the beginning some success and local European rule was set up in parts of Syria and Palestine, Muslims finally prevailed and in 1187 Saladin, the great Muslim leader, recaptured Jerusalem and defeated the Crusaders.

In spite of a Turkish-controlled administration and battles with the Christian forces, the eleventh and twelfth centuries saw a remarkable flowering of Islamic culture in Persia. It spawned such mighty scientific minds as that of Biruni who made an indelible contribution to mathematics and astronomy, as well as proving a sound historian. In the field of the arts the poet and astronomer Omar Khayyam was to write his famous *Roubayyat* and the philosopher Ghazali contributed much to Islamic theology. The Seljuk sultans also oversaw the building of hospitals and medical schools in most of the major cities under their control.

Once more any sense of stability was to prove elusive. The Seljuks were no more capable of maintaining supremacy than their predecessors and their power was slowly dissipated in favour of lightweight local dynasties. The only Seljuk sultans of any worth were Malik Shah who reigned from 1072 until 1092 and his predecessor Alp Arslan. The latter had achieved a significant victory over the forces of the Byzantine emperor at the Battle of Malazgirt in 1071 after which he was able to bring Anatolia (modern Turkey) under Muslim control. It was this advance, coming dangerously close to the heartlands of the Byzantine Christian Empire that proved one of the major factors in Pope Urban's decision to mount the First Crusade. But the leaders who came in the wake of Alp Arslan and Malik Shah were often weak and ineffectual men and the dynasty ended in 1194 when the last sultan was slain in battle. The only notable success among the petty states that rose and fell during the period was that of Khorasan whose hegemony briefly extended from the borders of China to Afghanistan.

Below: *A medieval portrait of the emperor Saladin.*

None among the Seljuks had reckoned, however, on the ambitions of a formidable Asian warrior named Temujin, better known by the title he adopted in 1206, "Emperor of All" or Genghis Khan. Temujin had effectively united the nomadic tribes of the Siberian steppes, the Mongols, and built a reputation as a merciless and bloodthirsty conqueror directing highly mobile troops of cavalry known as *ordus*, from whence came the term "Mongol hordes". He directed his attention first to subduing China and then turned to the west, advancing through Afghanistan, Persia and southern Russia. The end came for the Muslim Empire when a Mongol general named Hulagu captured Baghdad in 1258. He reduced much of the city to rubble, destroying its culture, including its incomparable libraries.

In Anatolia the Sultanate of Rum managed to hold out against the odds until 1240. Meanwhile in North Africa, various local dynasties held sway until two powerful Berber clans succeeded in uniting much of the area and Spain in the twelfth and thirteenth centuries. After them domination returned once again to local dynasties, such as the Sharifids of Morocco who still rule in that country. In Spain the

Umayyads maintained control for another 200 years until they too weakened and were replaced by local power brokers. The last Muslim dynasty was defeated in Granada in 1492, bringing nearly 800 years of Muslim rule in the Iberian peninsula to an end. A Muslim caliphate of sorts was established in Egypt, based in Cairo and almost wholly symbolic, which remained active until 1517.

5 Qur'an

Most beliefs in a spiritual dimension to our lives become worked in some kind of formal system. At this stage they are called religions and are usually based on a teaching that the followers recognize to be the word and work of God. The teaching generally begins as an oral tradition and is then incorporated into the more permanent form of sacred and authorized books. Those who profess the Jewish faith identify the divine word with the Old Testament. Christians recognize it in the combination of Old and New Testaments that make up the Holy Bible. Hindus find it in the Vedas and Puranas. In Islam the most sacred book is the Holy Qur'an. Muslims believe not only that it contains a universal message for humankind, but also that it is a God-given revelation replacing all previous scriptures and, since Islam is the youngest of the great religions, the sentiment is easily understood. Yet many Westerners may also be surprised to learn that early chapters or *surahs* of the Qur'an share much in common with the Old Testament writings and that it recognizes such biblical patriarchs as Abraham, Ishmael, Moses and Noah, as well as Jesus and Mary from the New Testament. Abraham, for instance, crops up in no less than 25 of the chapters, his name recorded as Ibrahim, while aspects of Jesus' life

and work appear in 13 chapters. It seems clear from the amount of overlap in the narratives that Muhammad was familiar with both Jewish and Christian traditions when he lived in Mecca and that he was in sympathy with at least some of them, although others may have caused him concern. The Qur'an itself reveals a certain amount of ambivalence towards other faiths. That it owes a great deal to Judaism is clear from the amount of Jewish tradition it contains. On the other hand, between its covers, much criticism is laid at Judaism's door, alleging misdemeanours that range from concealment of part of the scriptures, enmity, hatred and Jews "hurting themselves by their own misunderstandings". In places the Qur'an leaves no room for interpretation.

Believers, take neither the Jews nor the Christians for your friends.
They are friends with one another.
Whoever of you seeks their friendship shall become one of their number.
God does not guide the wrongdoers.

(Al-Ma'idah: 5. 51)

In essence, however, the Qur'an dwells on God's relationship with humankind, reminding Muslims of His total command of their lives and the absolute necessity to submit to His will. The book is the earliest known work of prose written in classical Arabic and for many scholars it is, to this day, the finest example, unequalled in the sheer beauty of its composition, its cadences and rhythms. The reverence in which its imagery is held is demonstrated by the ways in which the text has been adorned in art and design in much

the same way as attention was lavished on copies of the Bible in past times. Calligraphers and illuminators have elaborated the words and verses richly since the first copies were produced and extracts from the text are incorporated into the design of a wealth of Islamic decor and architecture. Predictably this includes mosques but verses of the Qur'an can also be found in the embellishment of many public buildings, monuments and mausoleums. It was undoubtedly in part through dissemination of the Qur'an that Arabic became a world language.

Not only are the words of the scripture considered sacred but also the very fabric upon which they are written, so precise rituals are laid down for the handling of the holy book. Before touching the Qur'an a Muslim must go through the appropriate ablutions of his mind and body (see p. 104) and the book must never be permitted to come into contact with an unclean surface or be laid upon the ground. It has been suggested, not unreasonably, that the Qur'an in Islam is less comparable to the Christian Bible than to the figure of Christ himself as the Word of God substantiated. This makes the reverence attached to the Qur'an more understandable and begins to explain why any criticism of its sanctity or authority is regarded as blasphemy, tantamount to an assault on the very core of Islam.

Copies of the Qur'an may receive much attention and respect but it is essentially a work for practical use, to be read from and its words spoken aloud. Qur'an in Arabic means, literally, "recital" and an important part of a practising Muslim's daily activity includes recitation of *surahs* (surats), each of which commences with the dedication, "In the Name of Allah, the Compassionate, the Merciful" and which is

بود دست عیسی علیه السلام مکرم بندۀ کی ما روی

بیکوهی کرده ایم و وزرا منصب پیغامبری رسانیدیک

و او را مثلی کرده ام برای بنی اسرائیل نا بود دلیل که

هر قدرت و حکمت کی آدمی زاده بی پدر دنیا افریدیم

و و را بد نبد درجت رسانیدم و اکما خواهیم ملک کما

فریشتکان فرستیم کی اندرو ی من خلیفتان

بیک دیریا شنند چنانک سر ان نوب ادم علیه السلام

بودند

$$\text{وَإِنَّهُ لَعِلْمٌ لِلسَّاعَةِ فَلَا}$$

$$\text{تَمْتَرُنَّ بِهَا وَاتَّبِعُونِ هَٰذَا}$$

$$\text{صِرَاطٌ مُسْتَقِيمٌ وَلَا}$$

then further divided into verses or *ayats*. Reminders of the need for recitation come on various occasions in the text and such "recitals" can refer either to the entire work or to smaller fragments extracted from the holy book.

The reason for emphasis on the practice of recital, which a Muslim believes amounts to the most direct contact with the word of God, can be traced back to the very beginnings of Islamic tradition and to the Muslim understanding of the sacred origin of the Qur'an. The story goes that in 610 CE, during the month of Ramadan that was already holy in the eyes of Arabs, the angel Jibril (Gabriel) came to the Prophet Muhammad while he was sleeping and commanded him to recite the will of God, a miraculous task which, when he awoke, he found himself enabled to perform as if the words were "engraved upon his heart". The revelation of different parts of the scripture was to continue throughout Muhammad's life and it was his conviction that the *surahs* he had been commanded to memorize served to correct and replace all previously known divine scriptures including the Old and New Testaments.

The act of recital, known as *tajwid*, is at the centre of Muslim religious devotion and as a form of prayer it is by no means restricted to the mosque or the home. These days in the West one not infrequently sees a Muslim in a shop, an airport departure lounge or seated on a park bench reciting, in subdued tones, from his small pocket edition of the Qur'an. This may look odd in our eyes but it is incumbent on a Muslim to memorize various short sections of the scripture as

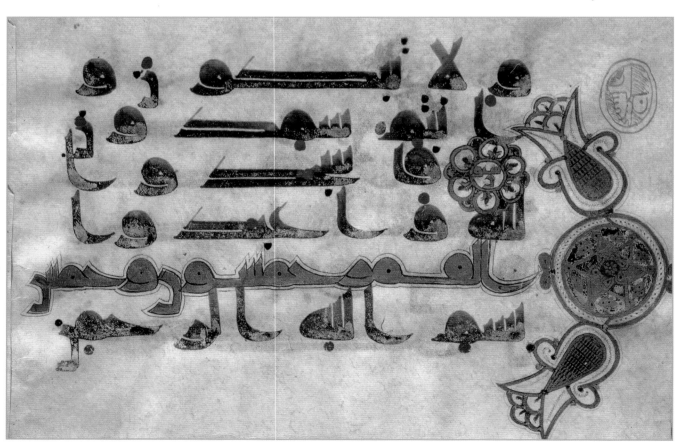

a child and to recite them throughout adult life during the round of daily prayers or salah (see p. 103). Other parts become familiar because they form part of the liturgy of ceremonies for special occasions, rites of passage such as marriages and funerals. Certain daily activities including embarking on a new venture also require blessings from the Qur'an and public meetings more often than not commence with recitations from selected *surahs*. In other words the Qur'an and its message amount to an indispensable part of a practising Muslim's daily life. In this respect Islam requires its faithful to have a fundamentally different response to that familiar to most Christians. For them the Bible is a book used in church lessons and is something which one may find on the bedside table of one's hotel room, courtesy of the Gideons. But at other times it tends to rest on the bookshelf unopened.

During the month of Ramadan, the ninth in the Muslim year and one devoted to fasting, each devout Muslim is also expected to recite the Qur'an from beginning to end, and in order to make this as easy as possible the *surahs* can also be divided into 30 parts of more or less equal length known as *ajza*, allowing the Muslim devotee to recite one part on each day of Ramadan. The depth of reverence in which the Qur'an may be held, however, and the importance attached to it in a Muslim's life is indicated strikingly in the number of individuals who succeed in the extraordinary feat of memorizing the entirety of the 114 *surahs*. Such a pious devotee is known as a *hafiz*, a person who protects the Qur'an in their heart.

Mere recital is not sufficient. As in most other religious systems, correct interpretation of the meaning of the divine word, not always clear to the layman, is equally necessary and a particular brand of scholarship exists in the Islamic world, known as *tafsir*, study of the so-called "Sciences of the Qur'an". Specialist theologians devote their lives to study of the *surahs* and to realizing the full implication of religious, social and legal issues they cover. This experience is a collective one, taking into account all aspects of the theology that have developed since the great age of Islamic learning, which flourished from about the seventh to the tenth centuries.

The exact origin and development of the Qur'an in its present form, as with so many sacred works, resides in the mists of tradition and antiquity and, these days, is the subject of considerable debate among academics. We know that during the lifetime of the Prophet no definitive version had been committed to paper and the *surahs* must have originated as oral traditions, memorized by the early followers of Muhammad. In centuries past the art of memorizing stories and relating them was much better developed than it is today. Popular tradition suggests that, under the first *khalifa*, Abu Bakr, the entire content was gathered together from a variety of written and oral sources and that this took place within two years of the death of Muhammad. An entourage of scribes to whom Muhammad dictated the verses had undertaken much of the preliminary writing while other chapters had been memorized by disciples. These individual documents and personal recollections, according to the authorized history of events, became the basis of the first definitive version of the scripture, the so-called Uthmanic Qur'an, named after

'Uthman ibn Affan, the third *khalifa*. During the second half of his reign, and by then about 20 years after the Prophet's death, 'Uthman commissioned the formalizing of the arrangement and content of the holy book into the work we know today.

Islamic scholars of that seventh century period are said to have been in general agreement about the Uthmanic version, but for a variety of reasons it was not slavishly followed in the early years of Islam. Problems arose in translation, there were different dialects to contend with among the Arab faithful and difficulties were exacerbated by the inferior quality of some of the calligraphy being produced. One of the major causes of discrepancy that arose involved a particular letter or script element being incorporated without any distinguishing symbols or marks, which meant that it could represent different consonants. The same vagueness could apply to certain vowels, the symbols for which may be totally omitted by the scribe of Arabic. The meaning of an Arabic word depends, however, on both consonants and vowels and such lack of detail allowed words to be interpreted in different senses according to local dialects. As a result at least seven versions of the Qur'an were recognized by one faction or another during the early centuries. It was probably as late as the tenth century CE (the beginning of the fourth century in Islamic reckoning) that sufficient improvement was made to the Uthmanic text for it to be accepted as definitive among Arabic speakers. Over the centuries the Uthmanic version has undergone a number of further improvements and the text recognized today throughout the world is the Egyptian edition published in 1924. This includes all necessary grammatical and pronunciation details, so that even someone not familiar with Arabic can use it effectively.

Such is the conventional view of the origins of the written Qur'an. Documentary and archaeological evidence, however, now present a somewhat different picture, one that is strongly resisted by Muslim purists. It is a particularly sensitive issue because it questions the fundamental premise that the Qur'an known to us today is accurate in its reflection of the divine revelations received by Muhammad. Research carried out from the late 1970s onwards reveals that manuscripts from the seventh century when the first copies of the Qur'an were allegedly compiled do not exist. The defence has been put forward that the early copies have disintegrated with age but it seems unlikely, given the reverence attached to the work and the kind of evidence that has emerged from sites such as Nag Hammadi and Qumran, where Gnostic and pre-Christian Jewish documents have been discovered from much earlier centuries. Not only is there no evidence of written copies of the Qur'an from the Middle East, nothing has materialized from anywhere in the Islamic realms during the period within a century of the Prophet's birth.

Muslim scholars point to two early documents that they argue provide concrete evidence to the contrary – the *Samarkand* and *Topkapi* manuscripts. These, however, are composed in a script known as Kufic (relating to the city of Kufa in Iraq) which most academics agree was not in use in either Mecca or Medina during the seventh century and did not appear anywhere until late in the eighth century. During the seventh century the intellectuals of Kufa would have used Persian script and most scholars now consider that the earliest date for the two Kufic copies is at least 150 years after the time of 'Uthman. The oldest known copy of the Qur'an, about which scholars agree in terms of its age, is written in a script known as Ma'il. This type of script did indeed come into vogue in the seventh century and was in use in Mecca and Medina, but the copy has been dated, by experts at the British Museum where it is preserved, not to the seventh but about the end of the eighth century.

Whatever the archaeological and documentary truth concerning the authenticity of the Uthmanic Qur'an, a separate difficulty arose with the spread of Islam beyond the Arab sphere of influence, since the majority of people who have come to accept the faith do not speak Arabic. Muslim traditionalists argue that the original words of the Qur'an represent the word of God and that he purposefully

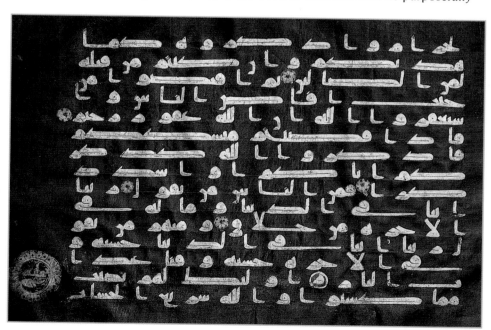

Left: *A beautifully adorned passage from a 9th-century copy of the Qur'an in Kufic script.*

did not deliver them in English, Urdu or some other tongue. For this reason the purists object to translation into other languages because such an activity constitutes imitation, a practice that is specifically outlawed in Islamic doctrine. Nonetheless more liberal thinkers contend that if the word of Allah was to be spread to the whole world it must be made available to other cultures. They point to various verses in the Qur'an that explain why the revelation was delivered in Arabic and suggest that some of these imply an unequivocal duty to translate the message into other non-Arabic tongues.

> We [Allah] have revealed the Qur'an in the Arabic tongue
> That you may understand its meaning.
> It is a transcript of the eternal book in our keeping,
> Sublime and full of wisdom. (43. 1)

There is some evidence that the liberals won the argument and that non-Arabic translations of the Qur'an were in circulation within 300 years of the Uthmanic version first appearing. This inevitably brought a fresh crop of problems over translation and interpretation of words. Modern Islamic students offer the timely advice that, even in its natural Arabic, the text will contain errors but stress that any translation out of Arabic immediately loses the official and perfect status of the work. For this reason, even though translations may be used for personal reference purposes, all ritual, irrespective of whether it amounts to public ceremony or private devotion, demands that the original Arabic words must be learnt and recited.

Below: Stone carved with extracts of text from the Qur'an in Kufic script.

The year 1972 saw one of the most remarkable archaeological discoveries of recent times during the restoration of the Great Mosque of Sana'a in Yemen. Workmen disturbed an unusual cache of manuscripts concealed between the outer and inner layers of the roof that are thought by some scholars to represent a kind of "document graveyard", a place where old copies of holy scriptures could be laid respectfully to rest. For several years until 1979 the pages, roughly stuffed into sacks, were locked away until a research project was organized by the Yemeni Antiquities Authority. It was then discovered that among the parchments were fragments from almost a thousand different copies of the Qur'an, probably representing worn-out or damaged books that had been removed from circulation. Some could be dated back to the first two centuries of Islam and it was quickly realized that these probably represented the oldest surviving copies. Since the beginning of the 1980s more than 15,000 separate sheets and parts of sheets have been carefully preserved with painstaking care and now rest in the Manuscript Archive of the Authority, pending more

Above: *Fragment of the Qur'an manuscript found in the Great Mosque in Sana'a, Yemen.*

thorough examination. As with discovery of ancient documents from the Jewish and Christian eras, such as those found at Qumran, there is considerable opposition from the Yemeni clerics to this kind of research progressing, since it may encourage a re-examination of certain sacred traditions. Novelty, as we have discovered, tends to be anathema in Islam. Nonetheless photographic copies have been taken of the fragments and are currently being investigated at the University of Saarland, Germany, where the main archaeological and philological work is based.

What especially captured the interest of academics and theologians alike was that several of the fragments began to reveal discrepancies from the known and authorized version of the Qur'anic texts. The discovery also raised deep concerns, since the differences confounded the premise that the Qur'an, as it has come down to us today, is perfect and immutable. Given the increasingly influential nature of the Qur'an in the modern world, however, many Islamic scholars believe it essential to look critically at these very early copies and the implications of what they reveal. The counter-argument is that that word contained in the Qur'an predates the existence of humanity and that to give the work a historical origin would be to make the entire Islamic struggle during the past 14 centuries meaningless.

In size the Qur'an runs to about the same length as the New Testament and contains 114 *surahs*, commencing with *Al-Fatihah*, the Exhortation. According to tradition this prayer was the first to be revealed to the Prophet Muhammad and it has become the most celebrated Islamic hymn of praise since learning it is obligatory on all who wish to study the Qur'an. It acts as a preface to the rest of the work.

> *In the name of Allah, the Compassionate, the Merciful,*
> *All praise be to God, the Lord of the Universe,*
> *The Compassionate, the Merciful,*
> *Sovereign of the Day of Recompenset!*
> *You (alone) we worship, and to You (alone) we turn for help.*
> *Guide us to the straight way,*
> *The path of those on whom You have bestowed Your Grace,*
> *Not of those who have earned Your wrath,*
> *Nor of those who have gone astray.*

Above: Two mullahs reading from the holy Qur'an in the courtyard of the Golden Mosque in Lahore, Pakistan.

The work closes with the *surah* called *An-Nas*, translated as "Men". The titles of many of the *surahs* seem rather obscure until one discovers that they received their names from more memorable passages they contain. The second in the generally accepted order of chapters is *Al-Baqarah*, which means "The Cow". This, however, does not mean that the *surah* focuses on the finer points of a domestic animal. It is arbitrarily given the title because it includes reference between verses 66 and 72 to the sacrifice of a young heifer demanded by God of the patriarch Moses. Otherwise its scope is too large, and the same is true of many other *surahs*, for it to have a title that comprehensively reflects the content.

Whatever the outcome of the historical debate presently gathering momentum, it is generally agreed that the authorized sequence in which the *surahs* (excluding the opening dedication) are arranged, beginning with *Al-Baqarah* and ending with *An-Nas*, is not that in which Muhammad received the revelations. For reasons that have never been fully understood, the chapters of the Uthmanic version were listed according to their length, in descending order so that the longest are now at the front and the shortest at the back. This convention has been upheld in all subsequent editions.

The *surahs* are said to have been revealed to the Prophet Muhammad on various occasions either during his time in Mecca or after he moved to Medina and by convention they have become classed as "Meccan" and "Medinan", though some in fact appear to be a combination of material, with verses from one source inserted into a chapter that is predominantly identified with the other. Those received at Mecca cover a number of aspects of the Islamic faith. Foremost among these is the message of the unity of Allah, the glorification of his name and the obedience to him demanded of all human beings. The earlier chapters also contain a historical view of the work of creation from the beginning to the anticipated Day of

Opposite: Students study the holy Qur'an at a religious school or madrasa in Istanbul, Turkey.

Judgement and an explanation of the form of the afterlife that a Muslim can look forward to.

Throughout the work the orator is Allah himself, who delivers his revelations in the first person plural, referring to himself as "We", apart from a limited number of verses in which either the angel Jibril (Gabriel) or the Prophet Muhammad speaks. These passages are recognizable because they are rendered in the first person singular. Thus one finds what might otherwise seem confusing switches of grammar.

> *This path of Mine is straight.*
> *Follow it and do not follow other paths, for they will lead you away*
>   *from Him.*
> *He thus exhorts you, so that you may guard yourselves against evil.*
> *To Moses We gave the Scriptures,*
> *The perfect code for the righteous with precepts about all things,*
> *A guide and a blessing, so they might believe in meeting their Lord.*
> *And now we have revealed this Book truly blessed.*
>
>   (6. 153)

Judgement Day features strongly in the writings. Of the first 60 *surahs*, only 13 omit to touch on the subject in one way or another and toward the end of the work one encounters some graphically written short chapters prophesying the final days of humanity's mortal sojourn. Surah 99 tells of the earth being shaken in her final convulsion:

> *When earth shakes off her burdens and man asks, "What may this*
>   *mean?"*
> *On that day she will proclaim her tidings, for your Lord will have*
>   *inspired her.*
> *On that day mankind will come in broken bands to be shown their*
>   *labours.*

In echoes of the New Testament book of Revelation, *surah* 100 speaks of the dawn arrival of the horses of the apocalypse, striking fire with their galloping hoofs. The following chapter *Al Qari'ah* announces the Day of Judgement.

> *The Disaster! What is the Disaster?*
> *Would that you knew what the Disaster is!*
> *On that day men shall become like scattered moths*

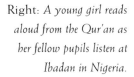

Right: *A young girl reads aloud from the Qur'an as her fellow pupils listen at Ibadan in Nigeria.*

And the mountains like tufts of carded wool.
Then he whose deeds weigh heavy in the scales shall dwell in bliss;
But he whose deeds are light, the Abyss shall be his home.
Would that you knew what this is like!
It is a scorching fire.

(trans. A. J. Dawood; Penguin Classics)

Yet the final pair of *surahs* adopts a calmer note, a plea to Allah for redemption. The Qur'an explicitly rejects the possibility of intercession by any intermediary between God and humanity.

I seek refuge in the Lord of Daybreak, from the mischief of His creation;
From the mischief of the night when she spreads her darkness;
From the mischief of conjuring witches;
From the mischief of the envier, when he envies.

I seek refuge in the Lord of men, the King of men, the God of men,
From the mischief of the slinking prompter
Who whispers in the hearts of men,
From jinn and men.

(trans. A. J. Dawood; Penguin Classics)

THE HADITH

No introduction to the Qur'an would be complete without looking into an important adjunct to the holy book. During the lifetime of the Prophet, his close companions allegedly elicited from him a collection of sayings and practices, the *hadith*, which became circulated as part of the early oral tradition of Islam. For example one *hadith* describes how a man "with dishevelled hair" came to the Prophet and asked him about the requirements of *salah* during the month of Ramadan. There follows a brief question and answer conversation during which an amount of practical advice is given by the teacher to the student.

Before the eighth century CE the *hadith* was passed from person to person exclusively by word of mouth and there were no attempts to formalize it into any kind of structured document. It was some decades before various authors decided to compile written compendiums of *hadith* but by that late stage, long after the death of the Prophet and when most of his contemporaries had also either died or been dispersed far and wide, it was difficult to verify which of these lists of sayings could lay reasonable claim to authenticity and which were imaginative fabrications. The problem of authentication compares with that experienced in the early Christian Church about which scriptures to class as canonical and which to be put aside as wholly fictional writings, often prompted by political or sectarian interest. In effect anybody, sane or otherwise, could claim to have met the Prophet and received advice from him.

It was not until the ninth century that learned opinion had sifted through all the known sayings, allegedly amounting to as many as 600,000, and placed them in groups of ascending credibility, evaluated on the basis of what they contained and who had originally recorded the information. Authorized *hadith* became known as *sahih*, literally "sound", and today two collections of *sahih* compiled by ninth-century scholars are regarded as particularly reliable. These include the *Sahih Muslim* and the *Sahih Bukhari*, though four others are regarded as canonical if of a lesser order of certainty. The modern collections, each containing about 4,000 sayings, amount to the main source from which the learned body of opinion, the *ulema*, draws opinion for the precepts of Islamic law. In this respect *hadith* amounts to the basis of *sunna* and effectively provides a second source of authority in Islam.

6 WORSHIP

FOR MANY PEOPLE WHO LIVE IN THE WEST AND who are not of the Muslim faith, two enduring images of Islamic devotion probably stand out above all others and both may seem equally puzzling. One of these is the cry of the *mu'adhdhin* (sometimes spelled "muezzin" or "mueddin"), the caller of the faithful, making his arcane proclamation from the lofty heights of a platform on the minaret of the mosque. The other is of rows of Muslims prostrated on their prayer mats, bare-footed, hands and noses to the ground, bottoms in the air. What does it all mean?

Such experiences are part of a carefully prescribed ritual of daily devotion that each and every able-bodied and sound-minded follower of Islam is required to maintain. This dedication to Allah is seen to be morally and spiritually

uplifting, as much a part of one's life as eating and drinking, waking and sleeping, and it represents the way of carrying out all aspects of living according to the will of God. The call of the *mu'adhdhin* and the position of humble supplication adopted by the faithful are among the more public signals of two essential premises of Islam: that the Muslim submits himself completely to his creator, Allah, and that the secular and non-secular life is inextricably entwined from birth to death. This is a difficult concept for a non-Muslim to grasp because, for many, the Judaeo-Christian religions have become increasingly abstract in their concept and detached from daily life in practice. The same concerns, it has to be said, occasionally occupy the minds of Islamic scholars in the modern world. As one commentator puts it, "It does appear we have turned everything in prayers to mere symbols and consequently many of us are marking time instead of reaping the benefits and rewards of our prayers." There is a constant exhortation to the faithful that true worship does not consist in merely reciting prayer several times a day, without the heart and mind being committed to an awareness of the presence of Allah, and to understanding and carrying out his will.

The non-Muslim also needs to be clear about exactly who or what the follower of Islam prays to, because there is a fundamental distinction between worship for a Muslim and, let us say, for a Christian. In Islam there is no sense that Muhammad is divine in the manner that a follower of the Christian faith perceives Jesus Christ to be the incarnate Son of God. Muhammad is merely the last and most definitive in a series of revelatory prophets or messengers who have been chosen by Allah in order to bring his word and command to humankind. Others, as we have seen in earlier chapters, include biblical figures from the

Previous page: A mu'adbdbin calls the Muslim faithful to prayer beside the minaret of a mosque in Teheran, Iran.

Opposite: Muslim women congregate en masse for prayer at an Islamic festival in Yogyakarta, Indonesia.

Below: A Nigerian Muslim at a mosque at Ibadan counts a string of beads between his fingers as an aid to prayer.

Old and New Testaments, most notably Abraham, Moses and Jesus of Nazareth. For a Muslim the divine revelations given to Muhammad and preserved in the Qur'an supersede all others. Nonetheless Allah alone is the object of worship and for this reason, a Muslim will strongly object to being referred to as a Muhammadan, a term that implies dedication to the worship of Muhammad.

Allah as an identifiable deity probably first emerged in prehistory among Nabataean and Arabic peoples and almost certainly derives in name and concept from the western Semitic god Il or El. The tribes of Hebrew origin that, in antiquity, came to occupy the northern part of Syrio-Palestine or Israel knew the universal God as El, a title distinct from Yhwh adopted by the southern tribes of Benjamin and Judah. The latter worshipped the same God who, tradition has it, revealed himself to Moses on Mount Sinai, but under an equally enigmatic "no-name", which translates roughly "I am who I am" and which was corrupted in medieval times to Jehovah.

Before the birth of Islam, Allah was perceived as the supreme deity, the creator of earth and water, within a larger pantheon of gods and goddesses. It was the Prophet Muhammad who identified Allah as the true and unique God, and who received his revelations. Muhammad also accorded God 100 names or epithets and all but one of these is listed in the Qur'an. Only the final name remains a mystery. To assist in remembering and reciting the 99 names, a Muslim may carry a string of beads, usually made from amber, which look similar to a Roman Catholic's rosary beads. These objects are thought to have originated in Brahmanic India where they are still employed in the worship of Vishnu and Shiva. From Hinduism their popularity spread first to Buddhism and then to Islam, with the earliest known reference to their adoption by Muslims coming from a ninth-century document. The medieval Crusaders are credited with having copied from their Muslim opponents and brought the rosary into Christendom. Though it has an essentially religious purpose, these days the string also serves as "worry beads" that men throughout the Near East and Mediterranean regions click through their fingers to calm frayed nerves.

For a Muslim, any sense of polytheism (belief in the existence of a pantheon of deities) is unforgivable and becomes the greatest of all sins. The doctrine of a Trinity of Father, Son and Holy Spirit provides, incidentally, one of the strongest objections that a Muslim carries about the faith of Christianity. The Muslim worshipper envisages Allah strictly as the absolute, transcendent creator and ruler of everything that exists and believes that Allah alone is pre-existent and eternal. Islamic tradition shares with Judaism and Christianity the concept of a world divinely created in short order rather than through a Darwinian-type evolution. The Qur'anic emergence of the material world from nothingness during a six-day period is referred to as *khalq*, although there is some difference of opinion among Islamic theologians about what was created first. Some scholars argue that it was light and

dark, others that the Pen preceded these emanations in order that the divine word and instruction could be inscribed at the outset of existence.

In ideas of eschatology, the principles of belief in life beyond death, Islam and Christendom also have a surprising amount in common. As in the Christian faith, the Muslim believer anticipates a day or days of resurrection followed by divine judgement, *qiyama*, when Allah will assess humankind for better or worse. This final apocalyptic moment in time will be preceded by "disturbances" on the earth and these will include the physical appearance of Anti-Christ who in Islam is known as al-Dajjal, the "deceiver" or false prophet. Tradition varies about the nature and purpose of al-Dajjal but he is described as a monstrous one-eyed character with the word *kafir*, meaning "unbeliever", branded on his forehead. He will, it is said, arrive from somewhere in the East (for some reason Indonesia is a strong contender) and will introduce a tyrannical reign of misery for either 40 days or 40 years before being overthrown by a *Mahdi* (see p. 166). Oddly perhaps, among mainstream Sunni Muslims one of the most oft-mentioned contenders for the role of divinely guided peacemaker and bringer of justice is said to be Jesus Christ, though in Shi'ism the honour is generally accorded to the occult twelfth Imam, the so-called Occultation or Hidden Imam.

Al-Dajjal is a somewhat demonic personality who, in Islam, is nonetheless distinct from the Devil or *iblis*, (derived from the Greek *diabolos*), known popularly as al-Shaitan or al-Rajim, "the one who should be stoned", and who equates with the unbelievers or *jinn*. In the Qur'an the Devil is portrayed as the angel who disobeyed God by refusing to recognize his own inferiority to Adam. In consequence he was evicted from Paradise but, as an outcast, he also brought about the fall from grace of Adam and Eve and continued in his ploys to lead successive generations of humankind into sinful ways.

Below: *Thousands of the faithful kneel facing Mecca in ordered rows at the Istiqial Mosque in Jakarta, Indonesia.*

According to Islamic doctrine, on the Day of Judgement al-Shaitan and his demonic horde will be consigned to hell-fire and the dead will rise up from the grave, not in the Christian sense but physically lifted by the angel Israfil who will also bring them before Allah to have their respective worth assessed. It is perceived that Muhammad will play an essential though not necessarily unique role interceding for the souls of his fellow human beings. In anticipation of this, after the call to prayer Muslim worshippers recite an invocation, which begins with the words, "O Allah! Lord of this complete call and prayer of ours, by the blessing of it, give to Muhammad his eternal rights of intercession . . .". Having been judged, souls will be required to pass over the narrow bridge that spans hell and while sinners will fall into the depths the blessed will enter Paradise. It is, however, believed that a short-cut to Paradise exists for those who die as martyrs in defence of the faith of Islam. This is one of the factors to which the enthusiasm for suicide missions among young and fervent fundamentalists can be attributed.

In daily worship Islamic devotion requires a practising Muslim of either sex to perform a round of prayers known as *salah* or *salat*, the only permitted exemption arising if the person is physically or mentally incapacitated. Yet the term "prayers", at least as it is understood by Westerners, does not wholly cover the matter because *salah* involves rather more of a closely meshed sequence of words and actions. In some parts of the world, including Iran and Turkey, the prayer ritual is known as *namaz*, but whatever name is used physical and verbal supplication is implied. *Salah* is also close to the Arabic word *silah* meaning "a link" and there is a strong sense that prayer opens a channel of communication between humanity and God. Throughout, it is pervaded by a sense of submissive request, the renewal of a covenant that brings guidance and moral strength to the believer. Among the opening verses of the Qur'an one finds the words, "You alone we worship and to You alone we turn for help. Guide us to the straight path". (1. 5, 6)

Ritual worship is performed five times a day and the sequence of five prayer sessions, an obligatory duty, is collectively known as *fard*. It includes *Fajr* in the early morning, *Zuhr* in the early afternoon, *'Asr* in late afternoon, *Maghrib* at sunset and *'Isha* at night before bed. Failure to perform any, or all, of this daily ritual round is a culpable sin and, as words of the *Fajr* devotion reminds the worshipper, "*Salah* is better than sleep!" In addition to *fard*, there exists in the Islamic liturgy a voluntary sequence of prayers known as *nafilah*. These include a special devotion, *sunna*, which the Prophet Muhammad used to perform as his customary practice regularly before and after each *fard*.

Salah is one of the so-called Five Pillars of Islam that, among Sunnis, are represented in the institutions of Islamic law or *Shari'a*. Each and every male Muslim in a sound state of mind and body is expected to follow this liturgy of principles from the age of puberty until death. In addition to *salah* they include *shahada*, the profession or formula of faith in which Muslims make the declaration, "There is no God but God (Allah) and Muhammad is his messenger." *Shahada* equates loosely with that which a Christian believer terms "creed" in that it is *aqida*, a simple, basic statement of commitment and faith in the unity that exists between Allah and the prophethood of Muhammad. In the eyes of most Islamic theologians today, if a person accepts the profession of *shahada* he or she may reasonably expect to be called a Muslim. The three other principles are *zakat* or almsgiving, *hajj* or pilgrimage, and *saum* or fasting. Symbolically the Five Pillars are represented by the design of an open hand with its five fingers, often to be found among the intricate carvings of a mosque. Anyone who visits the Alhambra in Granada, Spain, may be able to recognize the symbol if they look among the keystones that form the centre of the arch above various doorways. Shi'is regard recognition of the twelve Imams as a basic principle and, furthermore, some of the more extreme Muslim fundamentalists add the element of *jihad* or "struggle" to the Five Pillars, though this is not widely recognized as an aspect of Islamic law. *Jihad* is often interpreted to mean an "armed struggle" against the infidel, but when the term is used this context it is rejected by most ordinary Muslims.

The formula for *salah* is carefully laid down in Islamic law and requires the devotee to be in a state of mental and physical purity before saying his or her prayers. More than this, however, it is an institution that is arguably unique in religious experience aside from disciplines found in Buddhism and yoga. It demands the total harmonization of mental attitudes and physical posture and it is this symmetry of mind and body that is manifested in the actions of Muslims at prayer. In practice, as in other religious disciplines, perfect observance may sometimes fall short of the mark in pursuit of Islam. As one observer puts it, "I have seen Muslims who are in the habit of combining *Zuhr* and *'Asr* prayers for no reason other than they have no time to leave worldly materials to obey Allah. This is a popular phenomenon among students, especially those who care to pray." Generally though there is a stronger sense of religious propriety and discipline in Islam than in some other faiths.

Cleanliness before *salah* is essential and the demand that mind, body and clothing are rid of impurity stems from an assertion in the Qur'an that, "Truly Allah loves those who turn to him and those who care for cleanliness." The process is known as *taharah* or purification and it can take place in varying degrees according to circumstances. The

Below: A medieval painting depicts Muslim worshippers performing their ritual ablutions before salah.

lesser form is partial washing or 'al wudu, best translated as "ablution". This concentrates on the hands and the face and like so much of Islamic devotion it is performed in a precise, laid-down manner so that, for example, the hands are washed with clean water three times up to the wrists, ensuring that every part is treated, including the spaces between the fingers. The mouth and nose are also rinsed carefully. While 'al wudu is being performed, the Muslim preparing for salah also recites sentences invoking his God, "In the name of Allah, the Beneficent, the Merciful."

Total washing, the cleansing of the whole body, is referred to as 'al ghusl and is obligatory only under certain circumstances where the level of a person's impurity demands it. This can include entry of a convert into the congregation of Islam for the first time. For a woman, 'al ghusl is demanded after childbirth and, for both sexes, it must be performed following sexual activity. Clothing must also be subjected to the same rigours of cleanliness. Proper dress for salah requires a man or boy to be covered at least from the midriff to the knees (bearing in mind that Islam is frequently associated with parts of the world where daytime temperatures can be extremely high). For a woman attending prayer, the body must be entirely covered other than the hands and face and in some extreme fundamentalist traditions even the latter must be screened by the burqah, the all-enveloping gown that provides a fabric grille protecting the eyes from the outside world.

Above: A prince leads the faithful in Friday prayers at the time of the Mogul empire.

Following page: A fine study of Muslims at prayer by Jean Leon.

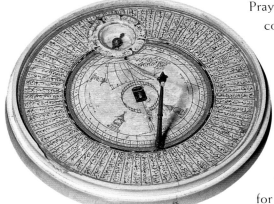

Above: *The medieval astrolabe was amongst the great Arab discoveries of the age and was used by astronomers to ascertain the altitude of the sun.*

Prayer for the Muslim believer or *mu'min* generally takes place as a communal activity in a mosque or some other meeting place and on Friday, known as *Juma'a*, the "day of assembly", collective prayer is a must. Friday in the eyes of a Muslim is not comparable to a Jewish Sabbath or a Christian Sunday in that these constitute biblical days of complete rest, though in the twenty-first century it counts as an official holiday in Muslim countries. Its significance is based on the divinely inspired command: "O you who believe! When the call is made to prayer on Friday, then hasten to the remembrance of Allah and leave off trading; that is better for you, if you know." On other days, however, and for the follower of Islam who cannot attend more formal devotion, perhaps because of work commitments or travelling, *salah* may be performed as an individual act. Under certain circumstances where the full round of prayer is impractical, the devotee is allowed to conduct a shortened version known as *salahul-qasr* and although it does not generally include additional voluntary prayer or *sunna* some Muslims perform both *salah* and *sunna* even while travelling. In any event, and whatever the circumstances, the underlying principles of ritual cleanliness and obeisance to Allah remain the same. So when a Muslim is seen, for example, getting out his prayer mat in an office or a railway corridor and going through the motions, he is performing one of the five obligatory aspects of *salah*.

Inside a mosque, the layout of the building is such that the worshipper knows that during devotions he or she is facing towards the Ka'aba, the central sanctuary of Islam and the focus of piety in the holy city of Mecca in Saudi Arabia. For the individual taking part in *salah* away from the mosque this direction-finding process is no less essential but may be more difficult without a map and a sense of world geography. It demands a certain amount of scientific expertise and at various times during Islamic history devices have been constructed in order to facilitate the exercise. Some of the simplest consist of small discs including a map of the world with Mecca at its centre and a list of carefully arranged place names. A movable pointer anchored above Mecca can be positioned over any of the places and its alignment indicates the direction in which the worshipper must face.

Group worship is, however, preferable. The call to formal prayer is known as *adhan* and the caller, the *mu'adhdhin*, must stand in his lofty vantage point facing in the direction of Mecca, his hands raised to his ears in line with the ear lobes. His words begin:

> *Allah is the greatest;*
> *I bear witness that there is no deity but Allah;*
> *I bear witness that Muhammad is the messenger of Allah;*
> *come to prayer; come to your good;*
> *Allah is the greatest;*
> *There is no deity but Allah.*

Following the first *adhan*, when the congregation are assembled inside the mosque, the call is essentially repeated, adopting the same hand gestures, though at a quicker pace and with less volume. Here it is called *iqamah*. The declaration *Allahu Akbar*, "Allah is the greatest", which starts all prayer is fundamental to the worship offered by each and every Muslim and is called *takbeer*. Without it no person's prayer is complete and in making the declaration of faith the worshipper, in effect, leaves the temporal world to unite with his creator. In the same vein, prayer finishes with the words *Assalamu, Alaikum wa Rahmatu Allah*, "May the Peace and Mercy of Allah be upon you".

The man who directs the performance of *salah* in the mosque is the *imam* or "leader" but the title should not imply an ordained cleric in the sense of a Christian priest or vicar. This is because in its early development, the "machinery" of Islam evolved quite differently from that of Judaism or Christianity. Beyond the instruction which is contained in the Qur'an there was no agreed formula in the sense of an "official truth" laid down by an ecclesiastical authority or Church hierarchy. For this reason terms like orthodoxy and heresy do not strictly apply in Islam, although it is fair to say that sectarian views differing from mainstream doctrine of *sunna* are often to be thought of as heretical and observance of tradition is always considered more important than change. The latter is generally termed *bid'a*, which translates as innovation or breaking with practice that has been built over a long period of time. Such a move is only tolerated if the *bid'a* represents a demonstrable improvement on the consensus of learned opinion. Otherwise it is bad, not in the sense of being false but because novelty runs contrary to Islamic religious principles.

An *imam* in Islamic society can be any adult male who has achieved a position of respect and good standing in the community. Even though he may sometimes present a sermon, it is not his job to impose any kind of dogma on the congregation but simply to organize and direct the process of *salah*. The nearest that an *imam* comes to taking an official post is when he may be placed on salary in one of the larger mosques. This is not, however, the only definition of an *imam* (see Chapter 10).

For anyone not familiar with Islam there also exists a confusingly similar term, *iman*. This, however, simply describes faith, the essential prerequisite for salvation in the life beyond death and which a Muslim believer is taught to understand in a number of aspects. These are essentially theological issues and are not generally of concern to the man or woman in the street, but they include three elements associated with belief in Islam. The first, *niyya*, refers to one's inner convictions and intentions as a practising Muslim. The second, *qaul*, describes the outward profession of one's faith. The third, *'amal*, has to do with the deeds one undertakes as a good believer. In the past there has been considerable debate over the comparative significance of one aspect against another and on the level of faith necessary for a Muslim to achieve salvation. Some schools of thought insist that, without *niyya*, the other facets of faith become meaningless.

Prayer for a Muslim is inextricable from the expression of humility and indeed one of the conditions for a believer to be able to go to Paradise is that prayers are

conducted in a humble and proper way. For this reason much importance is attached to the exact manner in which acts of supplication, including bowing and prostrating, are performed and these must conform with the instructions first provided by the Prophet Muhammad. As *salah* begins the worshippers are conventionally lined up in long rows and the logic behind this rather curious arrangement is that everyone is positioned as close as possible to the wall of the mosque that faces the Ka'aba known as the *qibla* wall. Hence mosques tend to be laid out as shallow oblong constructions. The centre of the wall contains a niche called the *mihrab* towards which the worshipper should face while at prayer, although in practical terms these recesses are often so small as to be invisible to most of the congregation and therefore have more of a symbolic than a practical value. The worshipper may offer one of a number of opening prayers of supplication but they must include the opening verses of the Qur'an, which read as follows (with slight variation in different translations):

> *Praise be to Allah, Lord of the worlds*
> *The Merciful, the Compassionate*
> *Master of the Day of Judgement.*
> *It is to You that we offer worship and it is to You that we cry for help*
> *Guide us on the straight way,*
> *The way of those upon whom you have already bestowed favour,*
> *And not those against whom your anger is directed*
> *Nor those who have gone astray.*

Below: The beautifully designed mihrab in the Jamaili-Kamali Mosque at Mehrauli, near Delhi, India.

Male worshippers repeat the raised hand gesture seen during *adhan* and *iqamah*, though for women in the congregation the position of the hands differs in that they are brought up only as far as the shoulders. This standing position is described in Arabic as *qiyam*. The hands are then lowered to the waist, right placed over left,

with words that begin, "O Allah, You are Glorified and Praised; Your name is Blessed; Your Majesty is Exalted and Glorified, and none has the right to worship but You". The supplicant bows in a gesture of reverence, placing the hands on the knees, and glorifies Allah from the first position of humility. This is known as *ruku* and it precedes the more abject position of obeisance referred to at the beginning of the chapter. This is *sajdah*, or prostration, which reflects total submission to the will of Allah and the very word "mosque" derives from the Arabic *masjid*, meaning "place of prostration". The members of the congregation adopt a precise position in which the knees, nose, forehead and the palms of the hands are in contact with the prayer mat and therefore touching the ground.

Even the feet must be correctly arranged. Each prostration for a man alternates with sitting back on the haunches with the palms placed on the knees. Women among the worshippers adopt a continuous upright kneeling position. Parts of the prayer are uttered aloud and others are recited in silence and each cycle of *qiyam*, *ruku* and *sajdah* is termed a *raka'ah*, a unit of prayer, the number of *raka'ahs* varying according to the time of day that prayer is performed and the circumstances of the individual. For *Fajr*, the prayer of early morning, it is two raka'ahs but three are required for *Maghrib* and four during *Zuhr*, *'Asr* and *'Isha*. At the completion of the *raka'ahs*, a prayer is made to the angels and then directed to fellow worshippers on the left and right for the peace and mercy of Allah. At whatever time of day the prayers take place it is expected that they should not be rushed through but performed at a sober and reverential pace. The realities and pressures of modern life, however, result in not all worshippers finding the time or inclination to pace their devotions correctly!

Above: *A more crudely wrought mihrab in a mosque in the Zarah region, Oman.*

As in a Christian service, formal *salah* may include a short sermon or *khutbah*, preferably no more than 25 minutes in length and often nearer 10 (the time that tradition maintains was usually set aside for such purpose by the Prophet). It is usually arranged in two parts, separated by a short intermission or *istighfar*. The *khutbah*, however, is not intended as an interpretation of doctrine but is essentially a speech that delivers hope and encouragement. It calls on the congregation to pursue virtue and reject vice, but with a strong emphasis on forgiveness as opposed to punishment. The person who delivers the sermon, known as the *khateeb*, is not necessarily the leader of prayer or *imam*, although the latter is expected to be the most knowledgeable about matters of worship The *khateeb* is required only to possess a reasonable knowledge of the liturgy, to deliver his sermon in a gentle, encouraging manner, and to be a man of both good standing and sound mind.

After the more closely regulated performance of *salah* each individual may enter into his or her more personal prayers, which are called *du'a*. These are spontaneous prayers that do not have to be performed at a particular time of day and are not expected to follow any kind of formal arrangement. Much as a Christian worshipper will find a quiet place in a church to kneel and say a prayer, so a Muslim will enter a mosque with the same intention. *Du'a* may be uttered silently in a position sitting back on the knees with the hands near to each other, palms facing upwards and fingers slightly bent. Special prayers may also be required for specific rites such as births, marriages and funerals. Prayers for a person who has died are expected of

everyone in the local community and in the funeral service a form of *salah* is offered that does not include *ruku* or *sajdah*.

An important facet of *salah* is the use and recitation of *hadith*. This provides a more practical interpretation of the teachings of the Qur'an, delivered by the Prophet Muhammad from his personal experience. It takes the form of a collection of the sayings and traditions of the Prophet in terms of what he witnessed and approved. These sayings are found in various books compiled by eminent clerics of the past. Among the most celebrated are the imams Al-Bukhari, Al-Muslim, An-Nasa'i, Abu Dawood, At-Tirmizi and Majah. Generally speaking though, it is the first two authors whose writings are deemed most reliable.

Aside from *salah*, devotion among the Muslim faithful may involve *zakat* or the giving of alms. *Zakat* means "purification tax" and is an obligatory charitable donation from the individual to the community or the Islamic state. It takes the form of a tax through which acceptance of one's allegiance to Islam is formally demonstrated. Currently each year Muslims who have a prescribed level of assets over and above their outstanding debts, either in the form of cash or commercial goods and commodities, must voluntarily pay 2.5 percent of such assets to the poor. A voluntary extension of this duty exists as *waqf*, literally "pious endowment", whereby an individual may leave money or property in trust for use in a variety of charitable needs, including such projects as the upkeep of a mosque, a hospital or a religious retreat. Because of the tendency in the past for wealthy property owners to abuse the charitable status of a waqf and establish it for the benefit of immediate families, Islamic governments today tend to cast a disapproving eye on such practices and also place genuinely charitable foundations under a degree of control by the centralized authority.

One of the most closely reported acts of Islamic obedience from the Western viewpoint is *hajj*, the pilgrimage to the holy places of Saudi Arabia. This remarkable event brings together tens of thousands of Muslims from all over the world in a single act of mass devotion. It takes place annually during the month of Dhu'l-Hijja in the period between the seventh and the tenth days of the month. *Hajj* is expected of every Muslim man at least once during his life and it involves retracing the footsteps of the Prophet Muhammad when he escaped from the birthplace of Islam in Mecca to the holy city of Medina. A man who is unable to make the pilgrimage for unavoidable reasons may send someone by proxy and the sacred journey is also open to women. Muslim wives may go with the permission of their husbands and provided that they are suitably chaperoned.

Last but by no means least among the five devotional Pillars of Islam is *saum*, the fast that takes place during Ramadan, the ninth and holiest month of the Muslim calendar. The dates on which *saum* begins and ends are not fixed but are based on the lunar cycle. This has only 29 or 30 days and so the exact period of Ramadan not only varies slightly in different parts of the world but also moves from year to year. The modern Islamic calendar includes a total of 354 during a 12-month period and so the beginning of Ramadan occurs about 11 days earlier each year and it rotates backward through the seasons in a 33 or 34-year cycle. In the millennium year, for example, Ramadan began on 27 November. The word Ramadan means "very hot" in Arabic because in the pre-Islamic calendar it always fell during the high summer. It managed to keep its place in the seasons since they inserted an additional month every two or three years to offset the loss of 11 days annually.

The fast is intended not least to bring home to the believer that many in the world are worse off than him or her, in terms of the basic needs of life. It represents another aspect of submission in which all adult believers must participate, except for those who are old and infirm. From the first sighting of the new crescent moon to the next new moon saum demands total abstinence from worldly activities including eating, drinking, smoking and engaging in sexual relations during each day between sunrise and sunset. Throughout Ramadan special prayers are recited after dark and the period ends with a joyous three-day festival that breaks the fast, known as 'Id al-Fitr.

Below: An unusual wall painting adorns a house in the Valley of the Kings at Luxor, Egypt depicting the hajj, or annual pilgrimage to Mecca.

7 THE BRANCHES OF ISLAM

WITHIN THE FIRST HUNDRED YEARS OF ITS FOUNDATION, the community of Islam was separating into distinct and identifiable loyalties. Many Muslim scholars dislike the use of the term "sectarian", claiming that since all Muslims are loyal to the teachings of the Qur'an and the *sunnah* it is unrealistic to say that the followers of the faith are divided. Nonetheless some painful lessons of history and continuing differences of opinion have resulted in clear distinctions and emphases. Each faction tends to view its own position as the legitimate one and regards the other as being unorthodox or even heretical, though the word "heresy" has no meaning in Islam comparable to that understood by Christians. The term "sect" is used here more for convenience than to define a separate doctrinal path.

SUNNIS

The Sunni branch of Islam has the largest number of followers around the world, supported by about 90 percent of the Muslim population reaching from the Arab heartlands, south into Africa and east through India, Central Asia and Indonesia. It is undoubtedly the most traditional or conservative of the various groups and it has effectively dominated the Muslim world since the seventh century after the small Khariji sect went its own way in 658, followed by the larger Shi'a movement in 661.

The term Sunni refers to strong adherence to Islamic tradition about the Prophet's form of worship or *sunna* and the full title of the movement is *al-sunnah wa-l-jamaa*, meaning the "people of the traditions of the Prophet". Sunni Muslims have always regarded the *hadith* (see p. 97) as a key element of the faith and it is from the hadith that the law or Shari'a was developed, a development made easier by the fact that the early rulers or *khalifas* (caliphs) had gravitated naturally toward Sunni membership during a period when the Shi'is lacked any formal administration and had a comparatively limited following.

Sunnis look to the body of religious scholars, the *ulema*, for interpretation of the law and, today, the most important seat of Sunni learning is the mosque university of al-Azhar in Cairo. In their understanding of doctrine Sunnis and Shi'is have three fundamental principles in common. Each recognizes the unity or oneness of Allah, accepts that the Prophet Muhammad received the divine revelations from God and believes that the souls of the dead will be restored to life at the Day of Judgement. Beyond this level of agreement, the two groups recognize the importance of different sets of *hadith*. It is, however, in the matter of the Prophet's succession that the main area of disagreement arises. In particular Sunni Muslims place less importance than Shi'is on the significance of 'Ali, the adopted son of the Prophet (see p. 119) and husband of Fatima, Muhammad's daughter. Sunnis reject the notion that 'Ali and his descendants were the exclusive executors and upholders of the traditions first laid down by Muhammad. Instead they claim that this role was taken by the *khalifas* who became the recognized leaders of the Muslim world but who were not necessarily elected from Muhammad's own clan. Unlike Shi'is they accept the legitimacy of the first four *khalifas*. Sunnis also attach major significance to the annual pilgrimage or *hajj* to Mecca while Shi'is hold other pilgrimages in the religious calendar to be scarcely less important.

Within the Sunni movement various smaller groups have evolved, ranging from the ultra-conservative Wahhabis to the radical and mystical Sufis. Between the seventh and ninth centuries several independent sectarian groups and four major Sunni law schools, or schools of jurisprudence, were founded and the tenth century saw the development of two more strictly theological schools. A further two independent sects, including the Wahhabis, were founded more recently in the eighteenth and nineteenth centuries.

The four law schools of *fiqh* pursue marginally different academic arguments. The earliest of the quartet is the Hanafiyyah School, founded in Kufa in Iraq by Nu'man abu Hanifah and still supported by the great majority of Muslims world-wide. The school resisted the power invested in the *khalifas* but ironically also earned their support. Its position is that the will of Allah is demonstrated by the universal consensus or *ijma'* of Islamic scholars and that the Qur'an, the *hadith*, *ijma'* and *qiyas* (roughly speaking analogy or correspondence between things otherwise different) provide the fundamentals of Islamic law, though the Hanafiyyah has also recognized the validity of certain local customs.

The next to emerge was the Malikiyyah School, founded in Medina by a local legislator, Malik ibn Anas, who also wrote the central plank of the school's argument, the *al-Muwatta* or "Beaten Path". The school concurs with its Hanafiyyah counterpart in most respects but originally insisted that the consensus of agreement or *ijma'* should be restricted to the people of Medina. Later this was modified to include the main body of the scholarly *ulema*.

The third school, the Shafi'iyyah, evolved in the ninth century under the patronage of al-Imam al-Shafi. He had studied the *hadith* under various scholars including Malik ibn Anas, but came to the conclusion that certain aspects of the academic argument were unacceptable. Later, al-Imam al-Shafi migrated to Iraq where he found himself defending his old tutor against considerable resistance to the influence of the Malikiyyah School. Gradually al-Imam al-Shafi began to win arguments among intellectuals in Baghdad and established his *fiqh*, collecting together the various principles of Islamic legislature and laying down the basic rules for their use.

The last mainstream school of law to be founded was that of Ahmad bin Hanbal, who had studied under various eminent legal experts including al-Imam al-Shafi. He made a detailed examination of the *hadith* and assembled no less than 50,000 such traditions in an extraordinary work titled *Musnadul-Imam Hanbal*. Nevertheless the Hanbaliyyah School came to be seen as reactionary, a hotbed of discontented fanatics who would not listen to the opinion of anybody outside their own strict ideology. Consequently the school failed to gain the general level of popularity enjoyed by the others and occasionally experienced persecution. More recently its principles have attracted the support of the puritanical Wahhabi sect and it is mainly active within the borders of Saudi Arabia.

Left: *A Persian painting from the 16th century depicts Muslims setting out on a religious pilgrimage.*

SHI'IS

Comprising about 10 percent of the Islamic faithful, Shi'a or Shi'ism constitutes not the minority group in the Muslim world but certainly a much smaller faction than Sunnis. Its followers, known as Shi'is or Shi'ites, are further distinguished into Ismailis and Twelvers (named after the first twelve *imams*) and are concentrated mainly in Iran, Iraq, Bahrain, Lebanon, Pakistan and India. In some of these countries, particularly Iraq and Bahrain, Shi'is actually constitute the majority of the Muslim population though they are still afforded "minority" political status because of age-old conflict with the Sunnis. The latter regard themselves as "orthodox" Muslims, many considering Shi'a belief to be "unorthodox" and therefore deeply suspect.

In order to understand how Sunnis and Shi'is came to go their separate ways, we need to travel back to the early years of Islam and the time of the death of the Prophet Muhammad. Up to this juncture all followers of the faith had been more or less united, though the Shi'a or, to give the full original title, the *shi'at Ali*, "supporters of Ali", were already displaying a particular approach to spiritual and moral guidance. But Muhammad's death in Medina in 632 left a thorny problem. Christianity had not experienced a comparable dilemma because Jesus Christ entrusted "the keys" to St Peter as his successor. But having seen himself merely the recipient of the divine word and the last in a line of prophets Muhammad had issued no such instruction and so his demise triggered a major debate about who would rightfully continue the mission. On one side of the divide were the Sunnis who argued that, since Muhammad had not appointed a successor, the word of the Holy Qur'an must stand as sufficient guidance for the Islamic community. To this they added tacit approval for establishment of the specialist body of *ulema* to arbitrate in matters of religious law and left it to the *khalifas* to safeguard the principles of Islam in government.

Others took a different stance, maintaining that the Prophet Muhammad had specifically identified his son-in-law and cousin, 'Ali (see p. 63), to be his successor. Shi'a doctrine differs, therefore, from that of Sunnis in rejecting the authority of the first three *khalifas* as guardians of the prophetic legacy. Instead Shi'is regard the *imam* as the main figure of religious authority, the infallible messenger of God irrespective of time and place.

Below: *Heavily veiled Muslim women in the tradition of the Shi'is during the Safavid dynasty. From a wall painting in the Iman Zahdah Chah Zaid Mosque at Isfahan, Iran.*

This arises from the notion that in completing the "cycle of prophet hood" Muhammad effectively closed the door on any possibility of further divine revelation. But in order to ensure that proper guidance of Muslims continued effectively after his death, he instituted a "cycle of initiation". According to Shi'a teaching Muhammad felt that his legacy could only be entrusted to a member of his own family and therefore he appointed 'Ali to become the first of the twelve venerated *imams* of early Islamic history (an interesting parallel with the twelve disciples of Christendom). 'Ali is seen to have occupied a particular place in Muhammad's affection. Not only was he married to the Prophet's daughter, Fatima, all the sons having died in infancy, he had been a staunch champion of Muhammad's vision of Islam during the Prophet's lifetime. The endorsement of 'Ali as rightful successor was taken to have been tacitly made when he became the adopted son of the Prophet and it was furthered during a sermon delivered by Muhammad at Ghadir Kumm shortly before his death in which, tradition has it, he pointed to 'Ali when he indicated that he was leaving to posterity "the two weighty things", the Qur'an and his descendants. Thus, for Shi'is, offspring of 'Ali from Fatima should properly lead the community and take on the mantle of *imam*.

The Sunni community emphatically disagreed and no clear consensus emerged, with the argument rumbling on until near the end of the ninth century, legal scholars and theologians wrangling over the form that an official doctrine should take. The situation nevertheless changed radically for Shi'is when the Abassid dynasty came to power in 750 and, as a result of persecution by Sunnis, the twelfth *imam*, Muhammad al-Mahdi went into hiding, an incident known as the "Occultation of the Twelfth Imam".

Below: *A Shi'a shrine south of Damascus in Syria reveals tile decorations with elaborate abstracted patterns based on flowers and foliage.*

During the era of the twelve, the sixth *imam*, Ja far as-Sadiq, occupies an especially important place in Shi'a tradition as the scholar who laid down the principles of the sectarian doctrine, but it is his forebear, Husayn, the third *imam* who was martyred in 680, who takes on the greatest significance amongst Shi'is. Supporters of the ruling Sunni-orientated caliphate, the Umayyad dynasty, by then based in Damascus, massacred Husayn and his followers near Karbala in Iraq. His death epitomizes Shi'a interpretation of the world — a sense of dispossession and martyrdom. The situation will only be resolved when, as Shi'is believe, the twelfth *imam* returns to complete the cycle of prophethood. In the mean time the guidance of the twelve is obtained through the mediation of clerics called *mujtahidun*, or "doctors of law", whose senior ranks, the *ayatollahs*, interpret the Shari'a or law and make religious rulings.

The historical picture becomes rather more complicated because of the further separation of Shi'a Muslims into Ismailis and Twelvers, again, a division brought about as a result of disagreement over a new question of succession. In 765 the death of the great-great-grandson of 'Ali and Fatima, Imam Ja far as-Sadiq, resulted in one faction, the Ismailis, offering allegiance to Ja far as-Sadiq's eldest son, Ismail. The Ismailis represent the dominant group among Shi'a Muslims and trace the hereditary lineage of their *imams* from Ismail directly down to the present incumbent of the title, Prince Karim Aga Khan, the 49th in succession. A rival group of Shi'is, however, the Ithna ashari, pledged their loyalty to Musa al-Kazim, the youngest son of Ja far as-Sadiq. They became known popularly as the Twelvers because they supported his descendants down to Muhammad al-Mahdi, the twelfth *imam*, who was forced into

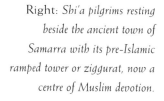

Right: Shi'a pilgrims resting beside the ancient town of Samarra with its pre-Islamic ramped tower or ziggurat, now a centre of Muslim devotion.

hiding. In their view Muhammad al-Mahdi remains in seclusion but will reappear at some time in the future as the bringer of perfect order and justice.

Irrespective of differences, the underlying message of Shi'ism is one of acquiring knowledge. Man must follow the path of divine awareness laid down in the Qur'an. Before he can hope to achieve salvation he must come to know his God and to understand clearly that all in the world of existence stems from an infinite source. By this token material values must be subservient to man, not the other way round, since all of these material things are ephemeral. The "reality" of today becomes the memory of tomorrow and the only lasting reality is Allah. Total submission to Allah becomes the epitome of human perfection and this is to be found in the example of the *imam*.

As was mentioned at the opening of this chapter, moderate spokesmen assert reasonably that, in the absence of an established Church, the growth of different communities and different interpretations within Islam does not amount to sectarian-ism and that there is no real divide between Sunni and Shi'a schools of thought. Nonetheless it would be facile to suggest that there is not a divergence, nor do all Muslims share this moderate view. Some hard-line Sunnis go so far as to claim Shi'a is a blatant heresy. A current site on the Internet entitled "Basic Shi'a Creed" under-lined with a crude skull and crossbones, proposes that "Shi'ism is a mixture of Zoroast-rianism, Hinduism, ancient paganism, Judaism, Christianity and Islam, wrapped up by Islamic terminologies".

Shi'a Muslims tend to focus on the aspects of suffering and alienation in the human condition. Martyrdom is an important aspect of their faith and the search for answers to these matters relies on a more esoteric interpretation of the *Shari'a* and the Qur'an than that of Sunnis. Yet interest in martyrdom extends beyond the Shi'a sphere of influence and it relies on a verse of the Qur'an that states,

Above: *Detail from the medieval manuscript* The Fine Flower of Histories *by Loqman (1583) shows Muslim forces routing infidels before the gates of Jerusalem.*

Never think that those who were slain in the cause of Allah are dead.
They are alive, and well provided for by their Lord;
Pleased with his gifts and rejoicing that those they left behind
Who have not yet joined them, have nothing to fear or to regret;
Rejoicing in Allah's grace and bounty.
God will not deny the faithful their reward. (3. 169)

Martyrdom can refer to the spiritual martyrdom of ascetic deprivation but, for most people, it conjures an image of someone dying violently for their faith as part of a *jihad* or holy war. Notwithstanding claims that Islam is a wholly peaceable religion, the themes of the call to war, the call to martyrdom and the rewards of martyrdom are not hard to find in either the Qur'an or the *hadith* (see p. 97). The latter tend to place considerable emphasis on the benefits of martyrdom. Not untypical is a passage from *Sahih Bukhari*.

Allah's apostle said, "Someone came to me from my Lord and gave me news that if any of my followers dies worshipping none along with Allah, he will enter Paradise." I asked, "Even if he committed adultery and theft?" He replied, "Even if he committed adultery and theft."

(Hadith, Vol. 2, Book 23, No. 329)

If the Muslim believer is killed during violent conflict with the infidel, the benefits in the afterlife are considerable and they have provided encouragement for many militants during the history of Islam. The martyr is said to be granted a short-cut to the highest ranks among the souls in Paradise where the *dar al-shuhada*, the House of Martyrs, is seen as the most beautiful place in which to spend eternity. En route such a martyred soul qualifies to avoid any kind of intervening purgatory or *barzakh*, since the act of giving one's life in defence of the faith frees the spirit from all taint of sin. It is this glorious vision that motivates extremists to embark on the suicide missions that have captured so many grim headlines in recent times. The majority of moderate Muslims do not identify with such sentiments but leaders of Islamic resistance movements emphasize that death in the cause of one's God, even if it is voluntary, cannot be suicide if the act kills an enemy.

KHARIJIS

The smallest of the three factions of Islam, Kharijis or, as their descendants are known today, Ibadis, make up at most 1 percent of the worldwide Muslim community. They are found mainly in Oman where they are the dominant group, accounting for 43 percent of the population, with Sunnis at 28 percent and Hindus and Christians making up the remainder. Smaller communities of Kharijis are also located in the north-western part of Libya, the Jerba region of Tunisia and parts of southern Algeria and East Africa. These surviving devotees do not descend from the original breakaway movement but from a moderate branch founded around 700 by Abdullah ibn Ibad from whose inspiration the title Ibadi derives.

The first Kharijis (meaning of "those who left"), officially separated from the body of Sunni Islam in 658 in the wake of the assassination of *khalifa* 'Uthman ibn Affan two years earlier and his replacement by 'Ali, the son-in-law of the Prophet. They opposed the Umayyad dynasty of 'Uthman, arguing that 'Umar had been the last authorized *khalifa*, but also rejected the Shi'a claim of legitimacy for 'Ali or any other descendants of the Prophet Muhammad to govern the Islamic community, preaching that anyone could take the role providing that he had earned popular support. In effect they represented the first Islamic anarchists, denying any authority other than their own rather flexible and inconsistent set of rules. In their argument the word substantiated in the Qur'an is divine and man should not therefore judge upon it, nor should human arbitrators decide on the legitimacy of the actions of others.

Tribal factions of Kharijis appeared on the streets and delivered a strict fundamentalist message of morality. They called on undeniable literary talents to generate anarchist poetry and stir up dissent but this overtly peaceful approach was often backed by violent assaults on those who did not support them. They regarded everyone else as an infidel or unbeliever and refused contact with strangers. They also maintained, in seeming contradiction, that all races are equal in the eyes of Allah and that there should be no distinction between Arabs and non-Arabs, a form of socialism that earned them many supporters in the early days when other Muslims were taking a more disparaging view of other races.

In 680 Mecca was retaken by the Umayyads and Kharijis were scattered to the more remote areas of the Arabian peninsula and beyond. Their radical influence dwindled and they were persecuted by the Umayyad *khalifas*. Other than in limited pockets of solidarity they had virtually ceased to exist as a militant sect by 750, and became regarded more as a nuisance strand of fringe intellect.

SUFI

No journey through the sometimes confusing forms of Islam would be complete without a pause to consider Sufism, the most mystical and ascetic aspect of the faith. That this is a discipline of bodily and material denial, the pursuit of austerity in order to discover the true spiritual path, is made clear in the name of the movement. *Sufis* means "wearers of wool" and refers to the rough and not especially comfortable garments favoured by ascetics as penitential shirts. For a follower of Sufism the way of inner meditation or *tariqa* holds greater importance than the outward path of following the *Shari'a* law.

Below: *Sufis dance at Sa'adi, Shiraz Tomb.*

Even during the lifetime of the Prophet certain converts to Islam were not satisfied with merely following his visionary path and teaching but needed to find a closer relationship to God and they did this through a discipline observed by men of similar persuasion in other faiths, that of bodily denial and withdrawal from the world of the flesh. Like Kharijis they tended towards anarchy. The attention of Muslims was probably first drawn to the ascetic way of life practised by hermits of the Eastern Christian churches but was modified to suit the framework of orthodox Islam. As in some examples of Christian mysticism, that of the Sufis focuses on the unworldly nature of God. Some claim that the first person to be known as a Sufi was abu Hashim who lived in Kufa during the middle of the eighth century but the movement was growing between the seventh and ninth centuries, during which the most notable Arabian pioneers included al-Hasan al Basri and al-Muhasibi. Its roots are said to be in the southern Iraqi city of Basra. Members either withdrew from society as recluses or set about following a more devout lifestyle in the community. If there is an exception to the general style of Sufism it is to be found amongst certain Sufi groups practising in the eastern part of Iran, which has seen a degree of Indian cultural influence during its history. They subscribe to the unity of all existence and reject the dual existence of matter and spirit. God and the universe, everything that exists in nature, are one. The imagery contained in Sufism attracted several important Muslim philosophers, not least amongst whom was the Spanish mystic Ibn al-'Arabi (c.1165–1240).

Like Buddhists, the majority of Sufis follow what has been described as the "mystic path", a road that carries them upwards through levels of worldly rejection along which the material is replaced by ever-increasing spiritual awareness. They gain much of their inspiration through poetry and music while also turning to the more mystical elements found in the Qur'an such as Muhammad's transportation to heaven from Jerusalem. On the other hand there is little to be found in the

Above: *The ascension of the prophet Muhammad.*

Qur'an that supports the ideals of Sufism and much of the learned and religious elite has dismissed it. Sufism has, nonetheless, spawned a number of outstanding creative writers, not least among whom was the thirteenth-century Persian poet, Rufi. While their talents in literature have bothered and occasionally inspired mainstream Muslims, Sufis have undoubtedly contributed much to the glory of Islamic art and their ritual dances possess a mesmeric and unique beauty.

For these reasons Sufis are less concerned with Islamic orthodoxy and the external observance of the Shari'a than with pursuing the ultimate aim of *ma'rifa,* true communion with and knowledge of God. Though an obvious contrast lies in their belief in a transcendental God with whom it is possible to achieve *hulul* or complete communion, Sufis share a goal closer to that of Buddhist asceticism in ideals such as *fana',* the elimination of the material self and literally the "passing away" into God, though this denial did not necessarily extend to celibacy. The ideals of Sufism not infrequently brought it into conflict with the learned body of orthodox Islam, the *ulema,* and in the early centuries several notable Sufis were condemned and even executed, not so much as heretics but because they were openly willing to flout the *Shari'a* law, claiming that they had risen above it. It required one of the greatest Muslim theologians, al-Ghazali, who died in 1111, to begin the process of reconciliation between orthodoxy and Sufism. He recognized that the abilities of the mystics, their heightened sense of perception or what was described as the "divine spark", added weight to the credibility of the prophethood of Muhammad. At the same time he set out to moderate the excesses of Sufis with a less extreme style of mysticism based firmly on accepted theology and a greater observance of the law. The result was a popularization of Sufism across a wider spectrum of Muslims, particularly the lower classes of society who discovered that it could provide a basis for community spirit.

As in most ascetic religious movements, after the first hundred years or so, Sufis began to proliferate into an assortment of schools or *tariqas*, literally "ways of inner meditation", staffed exclusively by men undergoing degrees of mystical initiation, starting with investiture of the woollen habit and working towards the full brotherhood under the tutelage of a *shaikh* known as a *ta'ifa*. Some may be loosely described as orders, though the majority of schools are run more as associations

Below: *Sufi dervishes accompanied by musicians depicted in a late 16th-century illuminated manuscript.*

based on the family of the founder. Many of the Sufi schools use music and dance in their rituals and it from this artistic tradition that the ecstatic dance celebrated by the "whirling dervishes" arose. The Mawlawi school in Anatolia (modern Turkey) that developed the extraordinary twisting dance routines was founded by Mawlana Jalal ad-Din-I Rumi in the latter part of the thirteenth century. The dervishes originally developed their dances as part of a ritual known as *dhikr* or "remembrance of God", though they are now performed primarily as a tourist attraction. In the past Sufis also practised feats of physical endurance, relying on the remarkable mental ability to withstand pain during such ordeals as walking over burning coals and being trampled under the feet of horses. Such individuals found that public demonstration of their abilities earned money from the curious and they gained considerable notoriety as *faqirs*.

Above: A portrait by an unknown artist of Mawlana Jalal ad-Din-I Rumi, the founder of the Mawlawi sect of Sufism, who lived from 1207–73.

Sufism attracted many from the ruling classes of the Umayyad and Abassid caliphates who found fulfilment in a life of withdrawal from material comforts. Members originally met and lived in communal houses or convents, variously called *ribats*, *khanaqahs* and *zawiyas*. Generally funded through charitable donation or *waqf*, these convents were used both for education and as missions from which Sufi evangelists were sent into the world. The movement spread from the Arabian peninsula into West Africa, India and parts of Central Asia where it has continued to play an active role in Islamic evangelism. Various Sufi orders emerged, included the Qadiris who were first active in Iraq but later found a more fertile spiritual climate in India. Others, such as the Naqshbandis and the Sanusis, were founded at different times in Turkey; North Africa saw the emergence of the Shadhilis, the Ahmadis and, most recently, the Tijanis. In the Balkans a quasi-military order, the Bektashis, has survived into recent times. At the outer margins of the orders "lay brethren" or "tertiaries" were admitted and some have provided spiritual retreats for women.

The most significant of the Sufi orders to emerge in comparatively modern times is that of the Babis. Founded in Persia early in the nineteenth century its membership was fired with romantic expectation that the *Mahdi*, the Hidden Imam, would soon return to lead the Shi'is into a new era of greatness and inaugurate a new prophetic cycle. Their founder was Mirza 'Ali Muhammad and in 1844 he proclaimed himself to be the *Bab* or gateway to the Mahdi. This immediately brought him into serious conflict with the upholders of *Shari'a* and he was executed in 1850 after various armed uprisings. The movement refused to submit, however, and one Baha'ulla, who convinced himself and his followers that he was the Twelfth Imam, took up the leadership. It is from his name that the more recent title of the movement, Baha'is, was drawn. Baha'ism is still active in Iran despite occasional clampdowns and its ideology of humanitarianism has spread with limited success into the Americas, Europe and Africa.

Today Sufism is practised mainly among older age groups of people living in isolated rural communities and is chiefly concentrated in Egypt and the Sudan. Its dwindling membership faces increasing problems in trying to blend age-old mysticism with the pressures of modern living.

8 HOLY PLACES OF ISLAM

THE CORE OF ISLAMIC WORSHIP IS THE MOSQUE, DERIVED from the Arabic word *masjid* that means a place of supplication. Like Christian churches mosques are often of great antiquity, sometimes dating from pre-Islamic times when they served other gods and during the early years of Islamic expansion the old Zoroastrian fire temples of the Persian Sassanids were not destroyed but adapted as mosques. In the Middle East the Muslim sacred places conform to a particular style and many of their features tend to be easily recognizable. Often they are possessed of immense architectural beauty and have been built without counting the cost. In the West, where mosques are often of more recent construction or are buildings that have been modified from some other purpose appearances can be deceptive, although even these still include certain essential features.

MECCA

Islamic tradition states that the birthplace of Islam is Saudi Arabia where the Prophet Muhammad was born in about 570 CE in the city of Mecca, a name sometimes written as Makkah. Muhammad received the first of the divine revelations that later became incorporated into the Holy Qur'an, in a cave on the outskirts to which he was in the habit of retreating to meditate. Little if anything is known of the place from pre-Islamic times, though according to an isolated and passing reference by the Greek Alexandrian writer and geographer Ptolemy, who lived in the second century CE, it may have been known as Makoraba. Situated in the western part of the country in the province of Al Hijaz near Jiddah (Jeddah), it is the place towards which all Muslims face when they pray, irrespective of where in the world they find themselves.

According to some Orientalists, Mecca lies at the junction of several ancient trade routes and has long been an important commercial centre. Some claim that it was a noted religious city before the coming of Islam and consequently that some of its sacred sites, since taken over by Muslims, have pre-Islamic significance, tracing back to early Judaism or the Zoroastrianism of the ancient Persians.

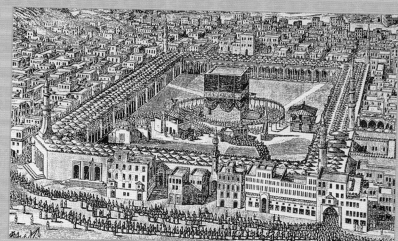

Previous page: An 18th-century engraving depicting the focus of Islamic devotion, the Ka'aba at the heart of the Great Mosque in Mecca, Saudi Arabia.

This conventional view is, however, strongly disputed by other scholars who claim that there is no demonstrable evidence of a pre-Islamic township at Mecca.

The central focus for all Muslims is the Great Mosque, al-Haram. To those of the Islamic faith it is comparable in significance to Jerusalem, Rome or Canterbury for Christians, though, as we shall find, Jerusalem is also a city of deep religious significance to Muslims.

The Ka'aba, the building sited in the courtyard of the Great Mosque and shaped like a cube (from which its name in Arabic comes), represents the most sacred core of Islamic worship. Shared traditions with Judaism are apparent in beliefs concerning the Ka'aba. Known as the "House of God" it is believed to date from before the lifetime of the Prophet and to have been built by Ibrahim (Abraham) and Ishmael. Ibrahim is, of course, regarded as the ancestor of the Arab peoples (see p. 20). Mythology has it that Ibrahim selected a place that had been sacred since a more arcane time as a sanctuary created by the earliest of all the prophets, Adam. Constructed of rough stone blocks the Ka'aba consists of a single windowless room, but the building has witnessed a number of changes since the time of Muhammad including an amount of enlargement, the construction of a mosque court and the recent addition of a solid gold gate. The Ka'aba is treated with great reverence and is washed ceremonially each year before being draped with a dark silk cover. The mosque also includes a sacred well, known as the Zam Zam, and, again, its traditions predate the birth of Islam because Hagar the Egyptian concubine of Ibrahim and mother of Ishmael reputedly used it to draw water.

Embedded in the south-east corner of the Ka'aba is the Black Stone, a meteorite supposedly given to Ibrahim by the angel Jibril (Gabriel). It possesses no religious significance nor is it thought to possess spiritual powers, but it is venerated as the only surviving object from the original building. Prior to Muhammad's time, the Ka'aba had been taken over as a place of pagan worship and was stocked with idols, but it was cleansed when the new faith took the city over. The Great Mosque is situated at the base of a valley where, from time to time, is has been vulnerable to flash floods after sudden seasonal rainstorms. In 638 CE floods did considerable damage to the original open courtyard of the Great Mosque and it was enclosed and extended under the direction of the *khalifa* 'Umar bin al-Khatab. A decade later his successors, commencing with 'Uthman bin Affan, undertook a series of building works that by 918 had resulted in an elaborate complex covering more than 30,000 square metres. This building was maintained without further alteration until 1955 when, following the wishes of the late King Saud, a project was undertaken to enclose the Masa'a, the sacred pathway that follows the ancient pilgrimage circuit and to incorporate it into the Great Mosque complex. This was expanded to an even larger size with the building of a series of octagons that radiate out concentrically from the existing structure. The design was completed in 1976, resulting in a sanctuary that could accommodate not less than 300,000 worshippers at one time during the *hajj*. Even this has since proved inadequate for the numbers of Muslims now visiting Mecca and further improvements were commissioned. In 1988 King Fahd of Saudi Arabia laid the foundation stone for a project that more than doubled the capacity of the complex. Finished in 1992, it can now accommodate more than a million people at any one time.

MEDINA

Second only to the Great Mosque is the Mosque of the Prophet in Medina (Madinah), the city to which Muhammad escaped in 622 after his life had been threatened. His final resting place is housed within this building in company with the tombs of his daughter Fatima and the second khalifa 'Umar. Medina is also a place of great antiquity, referred to in early inscriptions as Yathrib, although the Alexandrian geographer, Ptolemy gives it the name Lathrippa. Prior to 661, when the caliphate was moved to Damascus in Syria under the authority of the Umayyad khalifa Mu'awiya, Medina was the official seat of government in the Muslim world. In modern times the city became incorporated into the kingdom of Saudi Arabia in 1932 under the first ruler of the state, Abdul Aziz al-Saud.

As with the Great Mosque in Mecca, the Medinan Mosque of the Prophet has seen progressive enlargement over the centuries to meet the needs of an ever-growing number of pilgrims to the city, now more than three million annually. The work of expansion began in 638 under the khalifa 'Umar bin al-Khatab and today the complex is one hundred times the size of the original sanctuary at which the Prophet Muhammad worshipped. During the reign of King Fahd alone, the size has increased fivefold, to the extent that the mosque can now accommodate more than half a million visitors at any one time. The complex presents an impressive

Below: The final resting place of the prophet Muhammad lies beneath a dome in the Mosque of the Prophet in Medina, Saudi Arabia.

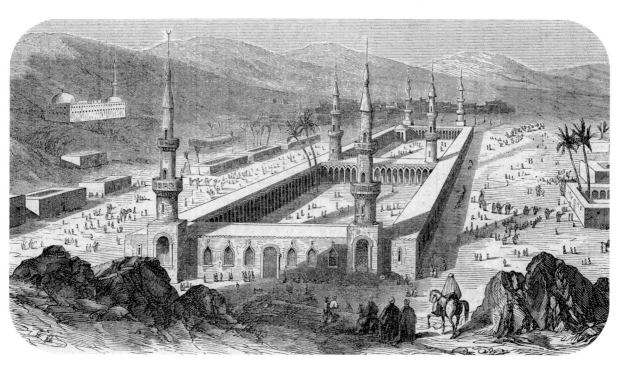

spectacle. It includes 27 domes and each of the six most recently constructed minarets is topped, 110 metres from the ground, by a brass crescent weighing nearly 5 tonnes and measuring 7 metres in length. As in the Great Mosque, the areas for public worship are today fully air conditioned against the intense heat.

JERUSALEM

Away from Saudi Arabia, Jerusalem occupies a special place in the hearts of Muslims as well as Jews and Christians. Known in the Islamic world as Al-Quds al-Sharif it is part of the land identified in the Qur'an as being "blessed for all human beings". Jordan was, in fact, the first region of western Asia to which Islam spread from its birthplace and it is where, historically, Islam first came face to face with the non-Arab world. Some of the closest companions of Muhammad are buried in Jordan, including one of the Prophet's adopted sons Zayd bin al-Haritha who is mentioned by name in *Al-Ahzab*, the 33rd *surah* of the Qur'an.

At the heart of Al-Quds is a complex known as Al-Haram al-Sharif, the Noble Sanctuary. At its centre is the Golden Dome of the Rock, the most celebrated Islamic shrine in the city, but the complex extends over 35 hectares, encompassing a marvellous combination of buildings, domes, gardens and fountains, all of which is thought of as a mosque. Said to have been commissioned in 691 by the Umayyad *khalifa* 'Abd al-Malik ibn Marwan, the Dome of the Rock commemorates the mystical journey undertaken by the Prophet in 620 when tradition has it that he was carried at night from Mecca to the rock of Al-Quds, from whence he ascended briefly to heaven. Muslims celebrate the event each year on a movable date during the month of Ramadan. The Dome is unusual for an early mosque in that it follows a strictly Byzantine ground plan, an octagonal design with a wooden dome, that was not generally adopted until several centuries later. The earliest dome buildings were actually developed by the nomadic Mongols, using animal skins stretched over wicker frames, but in Islam the mystical idea grew that a dome mirrored the architecture of the heavens and symbolism lent naturally to the construction of mosques. As the elaboration and opulence of the domes increased they came to epitomize humankind's desire to build a heaven on earth.

At the southernmost end of the Al-Haram al-Sharif complex, and connected by a walkway running from the Dome of the Rock, is the second most important mosque in the city, known as the Al-Aqsa Mosque. A little smaller than the Dome of the Rock and distinguished by a silver dome, it was completed in 715. In translation the name *al Aqsa* means "The Furthest" and it is so-called because of the Quran'ic verse that opens *al-Isra*, the 17th *surah*:

> *Glory be to Him who made His servant go by night*
> *From the Sacred Temple (of Mecca) to the farther Temple*
> *Whose surroundings We have blessed*
> *That we might show him some of our signs*

DAMASCUS

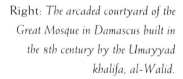

Above: *Ornate craftsmanship is revealed in the design of a window in the Great Mosque, Damascus.*

The early caliphate of the Umayyads moved to Damascus in Syria and, not surprisingly, many beautiful and ancient mosques are to be discovered there by the modern traveller. The Great Umayyad Mosque, one of the largest and most famous in the Muslim world, was commissioned by the *khalifa* Al-Walid early in the eighth century but the site was a holy place far back in antiquity. The earliest identifiable sanctuary there was founded at least 5,000 years ago and was dedicated to the Syrian god Hadad. In the first century CE, during Roman occupation of the city, the building became a temple to Jupiter and was later turned into a Christian church by the Emperor Theodosius in 379. After the Arab conquest, the building was shared by Muslims and Christians until al-Walid modified and enlarged it to its present shape and gave the Christians their own places of worship in Damascus. An immensely impressive building, the three gates of its main entrance are 20 metres high and in the main courtyard its richly decorated domed octagonal treasury standing on tall pillars makes fascinating viewing. The Christian connection can be detected in the name of the tower at the left-hand end of the *qibla* wall, still known as the Tower of Jesus and part of the prayer hall is also identified with John the Baptist. The building was badly damaged by fire in the late 1800s and the prayer hall was rebuilt by the Ottomans. Today, the scene that greets the tourist in the heart of the city and that symbolizes the extraordinary blend of cultural influences in Damascus includes two massive Corinthian columns that frame the Mamluk minaret built 14 centuries later.

The Great Umayyad mosque was copied at Quingjing in the Quanzhou province of China when Muslim influence spread there during the Northern Song Dynasty between 960 and 1127 CE. The mosque is one of the oldest to be found in China.

Right: *The arcaded courtyard of the Great Mosque in Damascus built in the 8th century by the Umayyad khalifa, al-Walid.*

Opposite: *The tiers of domes that characterise the beautiful Blue Mosque in Istanbul, Turkey.*

BAGHDAD

One of the earliest mosques in this capital of the old Abassid dynasty is the Abd Al-Kadir Al-Gailani. Built by Abu Said al-Mubarak bin Ali al-Mukharrami, the school attached to the mosque is more famous because of its association with his pupil, the celebrated Sufi mystic Shaikh Abd al-Kadir al-Gailani, who was buried there in 1165. The Ottoman Sultan, Sulaiman inaugurated the foundation of much of the current structure and was responsible for the construction of a superb dome over the tomb of Abd al-Kadir al-Gailani.

A tour of Baghdad's holy places would not be complete without a visit to the Golden Mosque, beneath the twin domes of which allegedly lie the tombs of the twelve *imams* and from which the whole complex grew. It has to be said, however, that other holy sites, including Isfahan in Iran, lay claim to be the burial places of at least some of the *imams*.

Baghdad also boasts one of the most beautiful of modern mosques, the Mosque of the Martyrs, that lies on the road out of Baghdad in the direction of the airport in a township known as Um Al-Tuboul. It is distinguished inside by its magnificent arabesques and glazed tile walls.

ISTANBUL

Of all the superb monuments erected down the centuries in the name of Islam, the Sultan Ahmet Camii in Istanbul, Turkey, better known to tourists as the Blue Mosque, must surely rank among the most glorious. Designed and built during the first decade of the seventeenth century by the architect Mehmet Aga, the building was inaugurated in 1616 in a ceremony performed by one of the youngest rulers of the Ottoman Empire, the Sultan Ahmet I who had ascended the throne at the tender age of 12.

Mehmet Aga had learned his craft under Sinan, undoubtedly the finest architect of the early Ottoman Empire and the builder of Istanbul's no less magnificent Suleymaniye Mosque. In just seven years of endeavour, Mehmet Aga created a magical artistic balance and harmony, to some extent emulating the style of the city's Byzantine cathedral of St Sophia, which faces the Blue Mosque across Sultanahmet Square.

From over the ornamental lake that borders the mosque, the visitor is greeted by a vision of six fluted minarets soaring skywards in slender perfection and framing a rippling cascade of lead-sheathed domes.

Passing through one of three huge gateways of the mosque one enters a serene courtyard roofed with domes and flanked by columns,

but it is the interior for which the building is justly famous. The decorations on the ceilings and upper walls are modern imitations of sixteenth and seventeeth-century floral and geometrical arabesques, but the lower walls still preserve original painted tiles produced in the nearby town of Iznik. Adorned with carnations, lilies, roses and tulips, interspersed with other plant designs including cypress trees, they are worked in delicate shades of blue and green and it is from these that the building earns its popular name of the Blue Mosque. Much of the original carved marble stonework still survives and even the doors of the mosque are individual works of art, constructed of wood inlaid with ivory and mother of pearl. The whole breathtaking spectacle is illuminated with light from more than 250 windows and, although the original stained glass has long since disappeared, much of it is now being replaced.

Above: *Detail of the fine floral designs that predominate amongst the tilework of the Blue Mosque.*

CAIRO

The Sultan Ahmet in Istanbul should not be confused with the Aqsunqur in Cairo. Found close to the Bab Zuwayla, north of the Citadel, it has also been dubbed the Blue Mosque because the facade is sheathed with blue-grey marble and the distinctive blue and green tile work lining its interior walls also came from Iznik.

Dating from 1346 and therefore notably older than its Istanbul namesake, it was designed and built in a cruciform layout by the *emir* Shams ad-Din Aqsunqur. In succeeding centuries the building largely fell into disrepair until it was restored in 1652 by Ibrahim Aga al-Mustahfizan who redesigned it in part to house his tomb.

Opposite: *The spacious interior of the Blue Mosque, Istanbul.*

Left: *A mu'adhdhin summons the faithful to prayer as he stand on the minaret of the Aqsunqur in Cairo, dubbed the "Blue Mosque" on account of its celebrated tilework.*

ISFAHAN

Opposite: *Superb architectural patterns created in the arrangement of domes of the Masjed-e Shah mosque at Isfahan, Iran, provided inspiration for the design of many other mosques.*

Among the holiest of places in the Islamic Shi'ite world is the city of Isfahan in Iran. The jewel in the city's central square is the Royal Mosque, known is pre-revolution times as the Masjed-e-Shah and marking the summit of Iranian religious architecture to which many other mosques in the area owe their inspiration. The sheer opulence of the building, built by Shah Abbas I with its foundation stone laid either close to the end of the sixteenth or at beginning of the seventeenth century, is unsurpassed. We know that the inscriptions found in the main entrance and created by the calligrapher, 'Ali Reza, date from 1616 but the complex is thought not to have been finished until about 1630. Statistics suggest that some 18 million bricks went into the construction, which was then decorated with nearly half a million tiles. The design of its splendid dome is typical of Iranian mosques and somewhat distinctive. It was copied in the construction of the Madrasa Mader-e-Shah, the Royal Theological College of Isfahan, completed in 1714.

The Masjed-e-Jomeh or Friday Mosque, which dominates the northern part of the city, is second only to the Royal Mosque. Tightly encircled by bazaars it is accessible other than at prayer times only by a flight of steps squeezed between busy commercial stalls.

The architectural principle of a dome supported by four arches and covering an area beneath, known as the *chahar taq*, is not only very ancient, coming from the pre-Islamic Sassanid period of Persian history, but is fundamental to the design of most

Right: *Intricate geometric patterns made from coloured glass and stone are revealed in a niche, high on the wall of the Masjed-e Jomeh or Friday Mosque in Isfahan, Iran.*

Iranian mosques that followed. Before the advent of Islam the basic layout of the Zoroastrian temple, a sanctuary within which a fire burned and which needed to be seen from all sides, conformed to the *chahar taq* and in later times this concept was extended to other aspects of design in the form of the *chahar bagh*, the formal gardens that came to encompass the pavilion and extend outwards from each of its four arches.

One of the more fascinating mosques of Isfahan, if for no other reason than its shaking minarets, is Monar-e-Jonban. The original *eiwan* or portico is thought to have been built in about 1316 to mark the grave of a hermit named Amu Abdullah Suqla and the two quirky minarets were added sometime later. The ratio of height and width of the towers, linked to the distance that separates them atop the *eiwan* generates an unusual sympathetic tremor in the structure, so that if one is shaken, the other does so in sympathy. Muslims visiting the mosque are permitted to experiment by grabbing hold of some specially added wooden frames and pulling on them, though this has resulted in a certain amount of structural weakening to the minarets and these days shaking is strictly regulated to avoid further damage.

MALAYSIA AND BEYOND

Not surprisingly Malaysia is well supplied with mosques. In the capital, Kuala Lumpur, one of the finest modern buildings is the National Mosque constructed in 1965 and faithful to a visionary design of Tunku Abdul Rahman, Malaysia's first Prime Minister. The building, of reinforced concrete with Italian marble finishing, comprises a subtle blend of traditional Islamic design and modern architectural technique. The courtyard is covered with an eye-catching fan-shaped roof made

up of 18 folded plates accompanied by no less than 48 smaller domes. The 18 roof segments symbolize the Five Pillars of Islam combined with Malaysia's 13 states. The main prayer hall can accommodate 8,000 worshippers and incorporates some strong Indian influence in its architecture, including white grilles reminiscent in their design of those to be found in the great mosque at Agra. The complex also includes a mausoleum to hold the mortal remains of Malaysian heads of state and it is topped by a minaret that soars dramatically to a height of 73 metres above a pool.

Today mosques are an increasingly common sight in non-Islamic countries around the world. Currently they are being built all over the United States, in conjunction with other Islamic centres and ranging from small, prefab buildings to grand monumental structures. California has no less than five and others are found from Arizona to West Virginia. Mosques exist in some unlikely places. There are at least seven in Ireland, including two in Dublin. The Regents Park Mosque is a familiar sight to Londoners. King George VI opened the first stage of the complex, the Islamic Cultural Centre, in 1944 on the site adjacent to Hanover Gate but planning permission for a mosque was not granted until 1969. The building work for this was eventually completed in 1977 at a cost of £6.5 million and provided two prayer halls, a library, a reading room and administration offices, with a detached residential block with the minaret. In 1994 an educational wing was added.

Below: Modern Islam is symbolised in the design of the Regent's Park Mosque completed in 1977 in London, England.

THE DESIGN OF THE MOSQUE

Essentially a mosque is a courtyard or an enclosed building large enough to accommodate those who enter it for worship, especially on a Friday, the Muslim day of communal prayer. Its alignment must be such that the faithful can face towards the Ka'aba in the holy city of Mecca and this direction is identified by the *qibla* wall in the centre of which is positioned a small decorated niche, the *mihrab*. It is mandatory that no doors or apertures are built into the *qibla* wall, although the other sides of the courtyard can have as many entrances and exits as are wanted.

Within this framework there are essentially two kinds of mosque. The larger, main mosque, the rough equivalent of a Christian basilica or cathedral, is a *jama'a* and is the place where Friday prayer is performed. Smaller and more local centres equating with parish churches are known as *masjids*. The latter term, however, with its anglicized version, mosque, is generally used to identify all Islamic places of worship. There exists a further distinction in that, while the *jama'a* tends to be non-sectarian and is frequented by Muslims of all persuasions, the smaller mosques are largely used by people supporting one branch of Islam or the other. So a Sunni will generally avoid a mosque frequented by Shi'is or Karrijis. In any event, admission to most mosques is barred to non-Muslims, who cannot wander into a mosque in the same open fashion that is allowed for a Christian church or cathedral.

In a mosque one finds none of the altars or other elaborate furnishings more familiar in a Christian church, a Hindu temple or a Buddhist temple, not least because of the Islamic prohibition on the imitation of the works of God. So, there is, for example, a total absence of images and paintings of religious scenes. Yet more abstract style of decoration is allowed and so the designers of mosques often incorporate resplendent patterns that are either strictly geometric in concept or based on plants but sufficiently impressionistic for the original form to have become unrecognizable. The exceptions in terms of fixtures and fittings include a pulpit known as a *mimbar* (minbar) from which the *khateeb* may deliver his sermon or *khutbah*. This stands adjacent to the *mihrab* and is reached by a short flight of stairs. An area known as the *maqsura* often encloses the *mihrab*. Formerly set apart for the private devotion of the khalifa or the civic governor, it may be protected by fretwork screens.

Outside this main enclosed area one invariably finds one or more towers or minarets, the number varying according to the grandeur and importance of the mosque. They are usually built up from the corners of the building and include a high platform on which the *mu'adhdhin* (muezzin) stands to call the faithful to

prayer. Aside from these fixed elements there are very few rules and regulations about what a mosque should look like.

The gardens surrounding the main area are, in some respects, no less important than the courtyard itself. Water and fountains play an important part in Islamic life since ritual washing is a necessary part of the devotion and prayer, so fountains and wells are generally to be found close to the courtyard or *sahn*, which is conventionally bordered by arcades or colonnades called *riwaqs* to protect worshippers from the elements. The Great Mosque of Sultan Hasan in Cairo, built in the mid-fourteenth century, reveals a Persian style of architecture where the courtyard includes more elaborated vaulted facades or porches called *eiwans*, the largest of which contains the *mihrab*. Elsewhere in the Arab world, mosque design tends to include a single *eiwan* connecting to the *mihrab*, while three cloisters line the other sides of the courtyard. The porch, in all its grandeur, thus serves as an elaborate link between courtyard and sanctuary, a transition point between mortal and divine. Additionally a mosque is not merely a place of worship but also a source of knowledge. It is therefore associated with a school or *madrasa* that may include a library and living quarters for teachers and pupils.

The inspiration for the fact that the essence of a mosque lies in its courtyard stems from the Prophet himself. The blueprint came from his private house in Medina built in 622. He used the courtyard, to one side of which stood houses for his wives, as a place of prayer and meditation. It was given a *qibla* wall, protected by a partial roof beneath which the Prophet and close companions performed their worship. At first this faced Jerusalem until the design was changed several years later and the *qibla* was orientated towards Mecca. In the decades immediately after the death of the Prophet mosques were simple and followed no particular conformity but then mosque building not only accelerated everywhere that Islam came to triumph but also became elaborated with additions such as the *mihrab* and the *minbar*. After some 80 years mosques had become elaborate and fairly form-alized complexes.

Most religions attach importance to raising parts of their places of worship towards the skies and this has been an aesthetic consideration in the design of the minaret, a slender tower that soars heavenwards, often to impressive heights. In its earliest form in the ancient Near East it was known as a *mil*, from which, according to some claims, comes the English word "mile". The first minarets, absent from early mosques, are thought to have been constructed in Tunisia in about 703, though the idea may have been copied from a Christian design since similar towers are found on early churches in Syria. Iranian minarets follow a different pattern and almost certainly they too derive from an old pre-Islamic style. The Zoroastrians, whose light religion of Ahura Mazda predominated in Persia before the advent of Islam, had first copied the *mil*, calling it a *monareh* or *monar*, with the literal meaning of "the place where light shines". Among their ancient places of worship that still exist is the *Atashgah* or "Place of Fire". Built of mud brick and reed it stands on a mound a few kilometres west of the holy city of Isfahan and perched on top at one end is a small distinctive tower, octagonal in shape and with arches perforating each side. Early Muslim planners converted many of these old Zoroastrian temples as mosques and retained the towers from which came the inspiration for the Iranian style of minaret.

As far as Islamic needs are concerned, the minaret is primarily of value to enable the *mu'adhdhin* to get above surrounding buildings and so make himself heard above the bustle of urban life, rather than walking through the streets like a town crier and announcing prayer as he had done hitherto. Designers also provided a high platform or *dakka* inside the mosque for the mu'adhdhin to announce his second call to prayer as well as a special desk for the Qur'an and a seat for its reader. The only other concessions to human need, aside from occasional reliquaries, included carpets, candles, lamps, stained-glass windows and incense.

Simple yet strict rules are laid down for entering a mosque. In a Christian church, convention dictates that a man takes off his hat while a woman leaves hers on and everyone talks softly. For a Muslim it is the shoes that have to go and the courtyard must be entered with the right foot, not the left. For Friday prayer worshippers are expected to wear best clothes and, surprisingly perhaps, are permitted perfume. Rules about women using mosques have been relaxed. In bygone times most mosques did not encourage

Above: *Moonrise over the minarets of the Rafa'I Mosque in Cairo, Egypt.*

Left: *An ornately fretted lamp, dating from the late 14th century and inscribed with the name of Sultan Hassan.*

Right: *Muslim worshippers must enter the mosque barefoot. Rows of shoes are deposited on the steps of the Omar Ali Saifuddin Mosque in Bandar Seri Begawan, Brunei.*

women to come to worship but to conduct their prayers at home and some forbade the presence of women altogether. Nowadays women are generally accepted in the mosque but have their places or times of attendance separate from the male worshippers.

One of the major departures in what evolved as the traditional design of mosques came in the fifteenth century. For a long time during the period of Islamic expansion when the Muslim armies were gaining ground from Christians, they took over Christian places of worship in much the same manner as Christian communities had adopted pagan temples in previous centuries. When the Turks captured Constantinople, a Byzantine city founded by Constantine the Great, they converted the great Christian basilica of Hagia Sophia into a place of Islamic worship. Hagia Sophia already possessed an open plan dominated by a dome and to this Muslim architects added smaller domes and minarets, removing any Christian artefacts and replacing them with glazed Persian tiles and other abstract decorations.

State rulers or other wealthy patrons generally build mosques but their upkeep is maintained through *waqf* donations and they form the focal point of Islamic towns and cities. When Muslim conquests have taken place, tradition has it that a mosque is erected even before establishment of a military camp and they are usually surrounded by shops, houses, schools, hospitals and law courts.

THE MADRASA

Schooling and religion in the Islamic world are more or less inseparable. From primary school age Muslim children usually spend several years studying and learning the Qur'an in a school that is attached to a local mosque. They then join a teaching group supervised by a scholar of the Islamic sciences before some of the more gifted students advance to the *madrasa* or college. Though not strictly sanctified places of worship, these higher institutions of learning in the Islamic world are intimately involved in the teaching and understanding of the religion.

Below: *Students walking through the courtyard of possibly the most famous seat of learning in the Muslim world, Al-Azhar mosque in Cairo, Egypt.*

Founded from the eleventh century onwards, often by sectarians such as Sufis, their pupils earn certificates, which in turn give them the authority to teach in a *madrasa*. Today these colleges have been superseded in many parts of the Islamic world by more secular universities and colleges, following a style of study that is familiar in the West, but in certain parts of the world, such as Pakistan and Iran, they still flourish.

The Al-Azhar mosque in Cairo is arguably the most famous seat of learning in the Muslim world, though it, like so many others, has experienced a chequered history. It was founded in 972 by the Fatimid dynasty and given its name, meaning the "shining one", perhaps in honour of Fatima the daughter of the Prophet. A college was added on and the first students were Shi'a Ismailis who enrolled there to train as missionaries but it was taken over during medieval times by Sunni Muslims who realigned its religious focus for the training of the *ulema*, the main body of Sunni scholars. In more recent times its strictly theological curriculum has been liberalized under the influence of such reforming voices as Muhammad 'Abduh. It admits women and its students may enrol for topics as wide-ranging as the scientific disciplines and modern Western languages.

9 MONGOLS AND OTTOMANS

THE MONGOL EMPIRE

IN ORDER TO GET A CLEAR IDEA OF THE CONFUSING events that took place in the Islamic world of the thirteenth and fourteenth centuries, after Baghdad and its tottering Seljuk administration had been sacked, we need to take a brief dip into the world of the Mongols. Brief is not an inappropriate description because although theirs amounted to one of the largest land empires in history, the Mongol *khans* held sway in Asia for a mere 168 years. In the overall history of Islam their intrusion therefore represents less a major upheaval, more a hiccup, albeit a bloody and tumultuous one. Yet, as with so much of Middle Eastern history, it is a period unfamiliar to most Westerners since it is rarely taught in schools.

When Baghdad succumbed to the Mongol forces in 1258 CE, Temujin who had styled himself Genghis Khan or "Great Khan" (as did his successors) had been dead for more than 30 years. During his lifetime, however, his fast-moving cavalry hordes of Mongol-speaking tribes had already laid waste to large swathes of Asia and Temujin had made the city of Karakorum in Mongolia into the capital of a huge centralized power structure. By the time that Genghis's third son, Ogadai, succeeded to the title of Great Khan the advance of Mongol power seemed unstoppable. In the east in 1234 CE the new overlord supervised the smashing of the northern Chinese Chin dynasty. In central Asia Turkmenistan came under the khanate of Temujin's second son, Jagatai, while to the west, Mesopotamia, Armenia and Georgia were being threatened. During the 1230s, the various Russian principalities were conquered one by one by the so-called Golden Horde.

By the early 1240s the Mongol armies had taken most of Hungary and were advancing towards Vienna in Austria. Their march was only halted by the news of the death of Ogadai, which encouraged brief retrenching to Russian territory while they decided who was to succeed him as the new Great Khan. After the short, two-year reign of one of Ogadai's sons, Guyuk, during which Pope Innocent IV became sufficiently worried about the state of affairs threatening the Christian realms that he wrote to Guyuk asking him to desist from further advance, the main khanate in the east passed for a longer period to a pair of Genghis's grandsons, first Mangu then Kublai. It was during the reign of Mangu that Hulagu, another grandson of Genghis Khan, took Baghdad in 1258, ending the power

Right: *Mongol warriors defeating German forces during the Battle of Leignitz in 1241.*

of the Seljuks, and it was he who instigated the khanate that effectively controlled Iran along with large parts of Iraq, Afghanistan, and Turkmenistan. With this the Muslim Empire and Islamic flowering was briefly laid low.

Having turned his military muscle on China and conquered much of its southern area, Mangu died in 1259. His brother, Kublai, succeeded him and after Genghis he is probably the best known of the Mongol rulers. Kublai Khan largely came to prominence after 1279, when he suppressed any remaining resistance from the Song dynasty in the south of China, and transferred the capital of empire to Beijing, known in his day as Khanbalik or Cambalu. It was there that, among others, he entertained the famous Venetian adventurer, Marco Polo. Once he had the southern part of China under his control he attended to the forcible removal of Tartars occupying the Chinese north and, of the countries in the region, only Japan and Indonesia managed to thwart his ambitions.

In theory the Great Khan now ruled over a domain that stretched from western Russia to the China Sea and from just below the Arctic Circle to the Persian Gulf. In practice, however, Kublai relinquished any personal claims to sovereignty beyond the borders of China and preferred to become the first emperor of the Mongol Yuan dynasty. A devout Buddhist he was a man of mercy compared with other Mongol overlords, for whom conquest and massacre had been virtually inseparable, and he made Buddhism the state religion of China. The policy of isolationism may have been a mistake, however, because within less than 20 years of this momentous pinnacle of Mongol supremacy, signs of weakness were appearing. Much of the Middle Eastern part of the empire had slowly accepted the faith of Islam and in 1295 the local *khan*, Ghazan, declared complete independence from Beijing. This was the beginning of a drawn-out process. As with so many dynastic empires that had gone before, that of the Mongols was destined to fail, not least because of Kublai Khan's policies of leaving other parts of the realm to their own devices. His death led to successive weak administrations and the Yuan dynasty rulers who followed him succumbed progressively to decadence in their Beijing stronghold. In 1368 the empire in China was wrenched apart by internal feuding, the *khans* were thrown out of office and were replaced by the Ming dynasty staffed with local strongmen. By the end of the century the western khanate in Iran had been broken up into small fiefdoms also effectively ruled by native stock.

The saga of Islamic fortunes in the thirteenth and fourteenth centuries was, however, even more complicated. While the Mongols were enjoying the limelight in the East, a new power base was poised to arise in western Asia, in what is now Turkey (formerly Anatolia). Although the Seljuk Turks had been defeated by the *khan* Hulagu they were by no means a spent force. By the close of the thirteenth century the western khanates were geographically distanced and politically more or less independent of the Mongol khanate in Beijing and the Mongols may have seen the Turks as a useful buffer against the forces of Byzantium, which still controlled western Anatolia. The Turks, who had arisen as nomadic tribes of horsemen in Central Asia, and the Mongol *khans* in the West had sometimes fought alongside one another and now shared a common devotion to Islam. Furthermore the interest of the Turks was not in fighting the Mongols but making advances westwards against the Byzantine Empire, which was becoming steadily more enfeebled as time went on.

Above: *Kublai Khan, the grandson of Genghis Khan.*

Below: *The explorer Marco Polo meets the Mongol emperor Kublai Khan in an undated miniature from Maudeville's Book of Marvels.*

The Rise of the Ottomans

In 1293 CE, from the melee of power-brokers in Western Asia, emerged a new Turkish tribal leader named Othman. Born in 1258 he was able to rally support of other local warlords, mainly because he controlled the tribal lands that lay nearest to the Byzantine frontier. Othman founded what was to become known in the West as the Ottoman Empire and with it Muslim interests in Western Asia and Eastern Europe were about to receive a much-needed boost. With the Byzantine military effort largely directed towards recapturing the Balkan states and Constantinople (sacked during the Fourth Crusade in 1204), the position of the Christian administration in Anatolia was weak. After more than a century of distraction with the Mongols, Muslims were about to resume their armed struggle against Christians. During much of the fourteenth century, Othman and his successors, Orhan and Murad I seized the strategic advantage and invaded large swathes of territory that had been controlled by the Byzantines. The process had begun with the conquest of Asia Minor. Orhan advanced on the city of Bursa a little way south of Constantinople in western Anatolia, took it and turned it into the Ottoman capital. A successful assault into the Balkans followed.

Part of the Ottoman strategy under Orhan involved an unusual but effective policy of recruiting children from Christian families in conquered territories. Known as *devshirme* it involved taking boys aged 8 to15 from villages, largely in the Balkans, and training them for state employment. The practice amounted to a form of tribute payment whereby these children were taken away and schooled as future administrators and soldiers. They were taught Islamic languages and Islamic religion. Those dragooned into military training eventually made up a substantial part of the elite infantry of the Sultan and became known as *janizaries* or janissaries. As Turkish slaves had become formidable warriors in the Muslim armies of the Abassids, so youthful converts from Christianity in time became much respected fighting men for the Ottomans. The policy also bore echoes of an earlier time when anyone who served the Roman Empire could technically call himself a Roman. By the sixteenth century, to be involved in the pay of the empire was to be termed an Ottoman.

Under Murad I, the Ottoman forces pushed north and west, skirted around Constantinople and in 1361 took control of the Anatolian region of Thrace, creating a second capital for the empire at Adrianople (now Edirne). This strategic move brought several benefits. It effectively isolated Constantinople from the rest of Christendom and, because it lay nearer to the new frontier, it provided an easier springboard into Northern Europe than would have been possible by marching across the Balkan mountains.

TAMERLANE AND THE MONGOL TURKS

The tribulations borne by the Islamic peoples through assault from Eastern and Central Asia did not end with the demise of the Mongol khanates. Murad I was killed in the Balkan campaign of 1389 during the battle of Kosovo, which saw the defeat of the Serbs, but not long after his death a new threat emerged from the East. This was a vicious henchman named Timur Lang, an Uzbek born in 1336 at Kesh near Samarkand, who had matured into a warrior hungry for blood and glory and with little regard for humanitarian considerations. Timur Lang, meaning "Timur the Lame" because his left side was partly paralysed, has become better known in Western history books as Tamerlane and he was destined to launch a new and even more brutal, if short-lived, empire. Although of Mongol–Turk descent, he was not related to Genghis Khan and while he may have been a professed Muslim he had no more regard for the welfare of the Islamic faithful in the states that he conquered than for infidels. His life was marked by extreme cruelty although also, with a degree of perversity probably down to more moderate image-seeking, by patronage of Islamic arts.

By 1364 Tamerlane stood at the head of a sizeable army in the Central Asian state of Turkmenistan, having seen off most of his rivals amongst petty chieftains and having made Samarkand his capital city. He falsely claimed descent from Genghis Khan, in order to give his position greater credence, and he began a series of aggressive manoeuvres that wrested control of Transoxania from former allies. He made clear that his ultimate intention was to restore the Mongol Empire to its former glory. For the remainder of the fourteenth century he lived up to his word, proceeding to wreak havoc in Iran, Iraq, Armenia, Georgia and Russia, advancing as far as Lithuania on the Baltic coast and operating a policy of slaughtering large numbers of those who had resisted him. In 1400, Baghdad once again fell to Mongol Turk troops. In the following season, three years before his death, Tamerlane rode into India. It was there that he is claimed to have committed his greatest atrocity when he took Delhi. Tamerlane is alleged

Below: *The Mongol warlord Timur the Lame, or Tamerlane, depicted during his invasion of India.*

to have massacred 80,000 defenders of the city, though the figure is probably something of an exaggeration.

Next, Tamerlane won a convincing victory over the Ottoman leader Bayazid, Murad's successor, and handed various territories in Asia Minor back to the local emirs. He died in 1405 while contemplating an invasion of China and was buried in Samarkand. His successors, the Timurids, maintained power in Iran and parts of Central Asia until the early sixteenth century but never again posed a wider threat.

Right: *The defeated Ottoman leader Bayazid I is brought before Tamerlane.*

OTTOMAN POWER REGAINED

The fifteenth century was nothing if not a period of complex military ebb and flow and Bayazid's son, Muhammad I, who reigned from 1413 until 1421, reversed the tide of conflict. Yet Muhammad I was better known as a good legal mind since he established a law code known as *kanun*. In this respect he was not offering new interpretation of *Shari'a* law, which would have contravened Islamic religious doctrine, but a tier of legislation that was wholly independent and fell outside the parameters of *Shari'a*. *Kanun* was segregated by Muhammad I into various rafts of legislation that dealt separately with the organization of government, of the military and of the working peasant population.

The necessity for *kanun* had arisen as a consequence of the ethnic mix that now made up the Ottoman Empire. The latter was by now a truly multicultural society, with its roots tracing back to Mesopotamia and Persia but also including the peoples of Central Asia and the Mongols from the East. *Kanun* stood, in effect, as a compromise between old Mongol–Turkish tradition that had relied heavily on imperial laws handed down by dynastic rulers, known to the Mongols as *Yasa* and to the Turks as Ture, and the strictly Muslim principles contained in the *Shari'a*.

Under Murad II, the ruler who followed Muhammad I, all the Anatolian lands once taken by Tamerlane were repossessed. At this juncture, the Ottomans decided that they had endured enough fighting. Murad II signed various peace treaties with potential antagonists, abdicated in favour of his 12-year-old son, Muhammad II, and aggression was temporarily suspended. This combination of circumstances, however, gave the Christian monarchs in Europe the encouragement they needed to resume the offensive. The Crusaders were ordered to launch a new crusade, on the risky assumption that the Muslim opposition had lost its stomach for conflict, but in the winter of 1444 the Christian forces were trounced at the Battle of Varna in Bulgaria.

THE FALL OF CONSTANTINOPLE

Muhammad II had been obliged to hand control back to his father during the crusade but when Murad II died in 1451, he resumed his place on the throne. Determined to live up to his father's reputation as a man of steel, Muhammad turned a speculative eye on Constantinople, at this time the capital city of Constantine XI, the ruler of the crumbling Byzantine Empire and a namesake of its founder. Isolated as it had become after the earlier Ottoman advances in

Anatolia and the Balkans, Constantinople was a prize ripe for picking and in 1453 Muhammad II placed it under siege, having first commissioned the forging of the largest guns the world had ever seen. For several months these massive artillery pieces blasted away the defensive walls with cannon fire and eventually Muslim troops moved into the city with little opposition. The operation against Constantinople earned their ruler the title Muhammad the Conqueror. In what was to become known as Istanbul Muhammad took over the famous Christian basilica of Hagia Sophia and converted it to a mosque and it was he who commissioned the famous Topkapi palace as his imperial headquarters.

Above: A 16th-century engraving records the Ottoman emperor Muhammad II besieging Constantinople in 1453.

Elsewhere his military adventures earned him less glory. His expansion into Europe was halted in Albania and, separately, at Belgrade. He also failed in an attempt to capture the island of Rhodes, which was to be held by the Knights Hospitallers until their final defeat in 1522. Muhammad II was not averse to trampling his fellows from among the Muslim faithful underfoot and during his reign he saw off potential rivalries from various Turkish warlords who generally ended their days beneath the sword.

THE CHALLENGE OF THE SAFAVIDS

Within the now increasingly powerful Ottoman Empire, the dawn of the sixteenth century witnessed, not for the first time in Islamic history, violence erupting between the Sunni and Shi'a branches of the Muslim faith and, for a while, this was to focus the attentions of the rulers on a crisis at home. It came in the shape of a family dynasty known as the Safavids who had come to a position of power in Iran and whose rule was to continue until the first quarter of the eighteenth century.

The Safavids had arisen as militant Sufis (see p. 124), their order tracing back to Shaikh Safi ad Din who died in about 1334 and who claimed descent from the seventh *imam*, Musa al Kazim. Converting to Shi'a Islam in the mid-fifteenth century the Safavids had been to no small extent responsible for the great flowering of medieval art in Iran. It was they who commissioned much of the fine tile decoration in Iranian mosques of the period. In 1501 under their leader Ishmael, and having built a formidable armed force known as the *qizilbash* recruited mainly from a number of Turkish tribes in Anatolia, they captured Tabriz, making it their capital city. Shortly afterwards they captured Isfahan and set about reforming Iran into a state once more run on lines of centralized power. By 1502 the Safavids felt confident enough to make increasingly belligerent noises in the direction of the Ottoman-held lands on their western flank. Not least among the causes of the ensuing conflict was the old enmity that had always existed between Muslims of different ideological thinking. While the Ottoman leaders were Sunnis, the Safavids were not only Shi'is but were keen to pursue a messianic path of evangelism. They were starting actively to convert Sunnis to their way of thinking.

At the time a timid ruler in the shape Bayazid II, the son of Muhammad II, led the Ottomans and so the administration made no overt response until after his death in 1512. His successor, Selim I, was a man of stronger fibre and he declared a *jihad* on the Safavid dynasty. He met the Safavid forces at Chaldiran in 1524 and robustly defeated them, taking over control of Tabriz. Having crushed Safavid opposition, at least for the time being, he turned his attention to the south and regained control over the holy cities of Mecca and Medina, extending Ottoman power as far south as Egypt. His wish in the longer term was to push the frontiers of Ottoman influence eastwards, since by this time in the sixteenth century the Portuguese were dominating the lucrative spice trade in the Indian Ocean and threatening Ottoman commercial interests. Selim I attempted to rout the Portuguese, albeit unsuccessfully, having authorized the building of a new Muslim fleet for the purpose at Suez. But sixteenth-century Muslim sea power was to prove no more effective than its Umayyad predecessor had been centuries earlier against the European naval forces off the coasts of Spain and France. At best Selim I managed to thwart total monopoly of the Portuguese over the commercial sea-lanes between Europe and the Spice Islands of South-East Asia, but the Portuguese remained as a potent force in the region.

Above: *The Ottoman leader Selim I defeating Safavid forces during the Battle of Chaldiran in 1514.*

Left: *An intricate blue faience design embellishing the dome of the mausoleum of Shah Nemattollah in Mahan, Iran.*

OTTOMAN DOMINATION

In 1520 Selim I died with little more to show for his years in office. It was his son who was to be instrumental in the Ottoman Empire reaching its second peak of power. Born in 1494, Suleyman I ruled the empire for 46 years, during which he was to more than double the size of the territories inherited from his father. He subjugated a considerable amount of Islamic territory including Arabia, on the argument that he stood as "defender of the faith" in a Muslim world where various dynastic rulers had all but abandoned Sunni orthodoxy. But this was not his chief concern. From the outset of his reign his eye was set firmly on the potentially unlimited territorial pickings available in Europe where he saw strong potential for destabilization of what was left of the Holy Roman Empire. It is interesting that at the time of the Protestant backlash against the excesses of Roman Catholicism, Suleyman invested massive financial support in the emergent Protestant countries. At the same time he saw that European rulers, particularly those of Russia and Portugal, nurtured expansion plans of their own and he was keen to minimize the risk to Islam from those quarters. On the political front he proved to be a shrewd and pragmatic man. In 1536 he formed a crucial alliance with France against the Habsburgs and this was to become a basis for Ottoman foreign policy until near the end of the 1800s.

Below: *A 16th-century painting records the arrival of the triumphant emperor Suleyman at Qasr-e Shirin in Iraq in 1639.*

What his father had commenced in the Balkans, Suleyman I finished in style and he became known in the West, not without some justification, as Suleyman the Magnificent. In a preliminary move after a few months in office his forces captured Belgrade as a useful stepping off point for the invasion of North-West Europe and a year later, in 1522, the Ottomans effectively found themselves in command of the eastern Mediterranean, having finally taken the island of Rhodes from the Christian Knights Hospitallers. Four years later he defeated the Hungarians at Bohacs. Within a decade Suleyman had Central Europe on its knees and, although he was destined not to take the city of Vienna, he stood threateningly before the gates of the Austrian Habsburg capital.

Suleyman I also turned his attention to the rumbling problem of the Safavids who still held sway in Iran, Iraq and parts of the Caucasus. He threw them out of Baghdad in 1533 and extended Ottoman control over most of southern Iraq but it would be another 100 years before peace settled on the Caucasus in the Treaty of Qasr-e Shirin made in 1639. That Suleyman I believed in his own omnipotence is clear from inscriptions he left behind. He described himself thus:

I am Suleyman, Servant of Allah, ruler of the world

My name is uttered in all prayers throughout the cities of Islam

I am the Shah in Baghdad and Iraq

I am Caesar in the lands of Rome

I am the Sultan of Egypt.

I took the crown of Hungary and gave it to the meanest of my subjects.

Left: *The Ottoman emperor Suleyman the Magnificent.*

Opposite: *The interior to the dome of the Suleymaniye Mosque, Istanbul, built between 1550 and 1557.*

In naval warfare Suleyman the Magnificent was less able to live up to his accolade. He never achieved any lasting success and if his naval fleet, under the command of a vassal, Barbarossa, became something of a nuisance in the Mediterranean, the Roman Emperor Charles V maintained the firm upper hand. In 1535 Suleyman was defeated by Charles at Tunis and was repelled 30 years later when he attempted to take the island of Malta.

Yet Suleyman's achievements were by no means limited to those of a military strategist. His name, the Arabic equivalent of Solomon, was well-chosen. He instigated a series of much-needed revisions to the *kanun* legal system first defined by Muhammad I and under his jurisdiction the secular legal code became known as *kanun-i 'Osmani*, the "Ottoman Laws". By and large *kanun* was now more important in day-to-day life than the *Shari'a*. To Westerners he may have been Suleyman the Magnificent but in the eyes of his own people he became known as Suleyman the Lawgiver. He was recognized as a generous patron of the arts and under his tutelage the Muslim world saw a great flowering of architecture, a new Golden Age of Islam. The period of his reign was marked by great architectural changes to the skyline of Istanbul. Undoubtedly his best remembered achievement was the creation of the glorious Suleymaniye Mosque in the city, designed by the brilliant architect Sinan, its inscription reading *Nashiru kawanin al-Sultaniyye*, which translates as "the giver of Sultanic laws".

Suleyman was responsible for sponsorship of many other building programmes including splendid mosque complexes throughout the Ottoman realms and he commissioned palaces, religious schools, roads, bridges, public baths and fine administrative buildings. He also sponsored aspects of the arts beyond architecture. Suleyman was an accomplished poet and composition flourished during the sixteenth century. He also employed some 30 painters in a royal studio, many of them from European centres of excellence, charged with executing scores of exquisite miniatures. Throughout his reign he managed to pick a number of highly capable grand viziers, including Ibrahim, Rustem and Sokolli, and these men were, to no small extent, instrumental in his achievements.

Below: *The 16th-century Suleymaniye Mosque in Istanbul, designed by the architect Sinan.*

Personal strife dulled the later years of his reign. Amongst his wives, the favourite seems to have been Roxelana but he had fathered children by several others and this led to jealous rivalries among the siblings. The eldest son, Mustafa, should properly have assumed the title of heir to the throne but it was not to be. Concerned that Roxelana was influencing Suleyman to consider her own children, Selim and Beyazid, for the succession, Mustafa gathered a faction of supporters that eventually posed a threat to the throne and in 1553 Suleyman made the decision to have him executed for treason. Roxelana's children then squabbled among themselves in a family feud that also saw Beyazid exiled to Iran, returned to Istanbul under duress and finally executed. The succession eventually passed to Selim II.

Suleyman I died while campaigning in Hungary in 1566 during the Siege of Szigetvar and his death virtually signalled the end of the medieval era of Muslim conquest. Although Ottoman forces were to take Cyprus in 1571 to augment their control over the eastern Mediterranean and under Murad III, who reigned through

the last quarter of the century, they took back the Caucasus region and Azerbaijan, they were also decisively crushed when the combined naval forces of the Papal States, Spain and Venice engaged them at the Battle of Lepanto off the coast of Greece. Although the Ottoman navy was rebuilt and dominated the eastern Mediterranean until close to the turn of the seventeenth century, the supposed invincibility of the Turks had been seriously undermined. In 1603 they lost all the ground they had seized in the Caucasus.

At the turn of the seventeenth century it was the turn of the Safavids to shine for a little under the hand of Shah Abbas I (1587–1629). He defeated some long-standing enemies in the north, the Uzbeks. He also took on the Ottomans, by now somewhat lacking in fibre, and reclaimed Iranian control over the Caucasus, parts of southern Russia and Iraq. At home he rebuilt the city of Isfahan and transformed it into the Safavid capital, doing what many had done before him in pursuit of popularity and a place in posterity by becoming a patron of the arts. He commission-ed the erection of fine mosques, schools, other public buildings and a bazaar in Isfahan. He also encouraged the native crafts of weaving exquisite silks and carpets, and did much to develop agriculture in the rural areas. Yet his dynasty was no more able to withstand the rigours of time than many others that had come and gone. His successor Shah Abbas II, by comparison with other rulers of his day, was a mild-mannered humani-tarian. He left little to show for his time in office and those who followed during the second half of the seventeenth century were, by and large, ineffectual leaders who, it is said, allowed women in their harems to dictate affairs of state!

The end came for the Safavids in 1722 under a leader named Shah Sultan Hosain, who is said to have expended more of his energies on seducing women and indulging his stomach than on administering the country. By this time the Safavid army, largely still recruited from foreign tribes and slaves, was no longer the force it had been under Abbas I and it fell victim to a surprisingly small force that descended from Afghanistan in the north-east.

As far as the rest of the Ottoman Empire was concerned, it was as if no one who followed in Suleyman's wake was able to live up to his standard of excellence. The days of glory when the Ottoman generals were allegedly able to put 100,000 horsemen into the field were past. A number of Suleyman's successors in the seven-teenth century proved either bad or mad. At the dawn of the seventeenth century a time-honoured bugbear that had troubled earlier Muslim administrations was nagging at the Ottomans, the need to raise money in both the public and the private sector. Inflationary pressures grew and with them corruption became the order of the day.

As Christian Europe expanded, the empire began a slow 300-year decline that was to end when its remnants were broken up early in the twentieth century. The final chapter for the Ottoman time of glory probably began in 1683 when they attempted once more to capture Vienna. The assault failed and it led to Russia and Austria stepping up not only their military response but also subversive tactics among non-Muslims in Ottoman-held territory. For a period of just over 40 years the Ottomans found themselves on the receiving end of a sapping war of attrition during which they lost much of their lands in Eastern Europe, while other parts of the empire openly declared political independence from central government.

The loss of territory had a knock-on effect. The sultans were longer in a position to recruit janissary recruits from the Balkans and the corps became increasingly decadent and anarchistic. Nonetheless, the Ottomans mounted several successful campaigns in the early part of the eighteenth century, notably against the Russians who were vying for supremacy of the countries bordering the Black Sea. The army of Tsar Peter the Great was defeated in 1711, Belgrade was taken yet again and, not for the first time, Vienna came under threat of Muslim assault. In the second half of the century an inward-looking Europe was too preoccupied with its Seven Years War to trouble the Ottomans greatly. Austria and Prussia vied with each other for domination of Germany and Britain and France locked horns in the battle for overseas supremacy in India and North America. But immediately following the cessation of hostilities, Russia turned its military attention onto the Ottomans, taking Romania from them, while Napoleon Bonaparte invaded Egypt.

The only serious attempt to revitalize the Ottoman administration probably came under the leadership of Selim III at the turn of the nineteenth century when he tried to reform the machinery of empire and the outmoded warfare techniques of the Ottoman armed forces. The reforms proved unworkable and he was thrown out of office. His successor Mahmud II might have halted the progress of decline when he set about the recentralization of government, had large numbers of janissaries slaughtered after an attempted coup and re-established the army on European lines. But the slide continued through the period of the three-year Crimean War that broke out in 1853. The efforts to resist French advances into Egypt resulted in the formation of an effectively independent Egyptian state under Muhammad Ali and decline in the north was pushed at a faster rate in 1877 when the Russo-Turkish war broke out. This had been triggered by the massacre of many thousands of Bulgarians in 1876 in response to a similar slaughter of Muslims by Christians. The Russians and Austrians concluded a mutual agreement and the guns of Russian forces were soon trained on the gates of Constantinople. In 1878 the Ottomans were obliged to comply with the damaging Treaty of San Stefano that effectively finished them as a political force in Europe.

By the twentieth century it was only the conflicting interest of various European states before and during the First World War that kept the Ottomans in power when they sided with Germany in 1914. The defeat of the Ottomans triggered a new mood of Turkish nationalism and the aftermath of hostilities saw the formation of a fresh administration under Ataturk, Mustafa Kemal. The sultanate was abolished in 1922, Turkey was declared a republic and by 1924 all members of the Ottoman family were forcibly removed from the country, thus ending six centuries of Ottoman Muslim power.

10 HOLY MEN & ISLAMIC LAW

MUCH AS CERTAIN RITUALS ASSOCIATED with Islamic worship may appear as something of a mystery to people living outside the Islamic sphere, so the titles of those holding responsibility in Islamic religious and secular affairs may also be difficult to understand in terms of what they do and why. The ear of the Westerner hears a confusing range of names including *mullah, ayatollah, imam, mahdi* and others. What do they mean? The answers are not always straight-forward because each term may possess more than one definition.

IMAM

Included in the chapter on worship is the outline of how an *imam*, in the modern sense, is a leader of prayer in the mosque though he is not necessarily qualified in any specific way, nor is he generally employed on a salary. The same title may also be applied, however, to an outstanding religious scholar, such as one of the founders of the four Sunni schools of law.

From the historical viewpoint, an imam can be one of the secular heads of the community from the early years after the death of the Prophet, virtually the equal of a *khalifa*, though Sunnis treat all the *khalifas* after the first four as being pretenders not fit to bear the name *imam*. In later times the title of *imam* was invariably accorded to those who professed outstanding religious zeal and knowledge. Among the best known of these men in history was 'Abd al-Qadir who gained great popularity among Arabs during the nineteenth century in the western part of Algeria and who fought a holy war against the French when the colonial interest of France in North Africa was being expanded. 'Abd al-Qadir was given the title *Nasir al-Din*, literally upholder of the faith, and his acknowledged mission was to restore the purity and integrity of Islam in Algeria. The conflict raged from 1833 until 1847 when he was defeated and imprisoned.

Historically, however, there is another meaning attached to the title *imam* that is of relevance primarily to Shi'is and in particular to those known as Twelvers, because it identifies the original leaders of the Shi'a minority descended from the family of 'Ali.

MAHDI

The twelfth in line of these charismatic leaders of early Islam is the so-called Hidden or "Occultation" Imam. Very little can be said with any degree of historical certainty about the personality of the twelfth *imam* and much relies on popular tradition that originates in words attributed to the Prophet.

> *The world shall not end until a man from my family and of my name*
> *Shall be master of the world.*
> *When you see standards of green coming out of Khorasan*
> *Then join with them for the Imam of God will be with there.*
> *He will be called al-Mahdi.*

According to Shi'a doctrine the full name of the twelfth and last *imam* is Muhammad Abdul Qasim, also titled al-Mahdi al-Muntadar, which translates roughly as Muhammad "the guided one and the awaited one". Twelver Shi'is believe that he was born in Samarra in Iraq in about 868 CE during the caliphate of the Abassid ruler, al-Mu'tamid. His mother has been named as Narjis Khatun whom some traditions place as the grand-daughter of the Byzantine emperor. Whatever her position, she was captured from Christian territory and taken as a concubine by the eleventh *imam*, Hassan al Askari. Almost immediately, however, one finds conflicting reports, in that one of the brothers of Hassan al Askari denied that reports of the birth of a child to Narjis Khatun were valid and claimed the imamate for himself. Wherever the truth lies, the tradition continues that, as a child, Muhammad al-Mahdi was kept in virtual isolation, presumably for his own protection, since opposing Sunni factions were strongly hostile to the claims of the Shi'a imams. He was paraded on rare occasions, in effect to challenge his uncle's claims on the leadership, but was otherwise kept out of the limelight until he reached the age of six. It appears that there was good reason for the secrecy because his grandfather, the tenth *imam*, had suffered a violent death and, likewise, his father was assassinated in 872 CE. The child who had inherited the title of twelfth *imam* was thus resigned to a life in hiding or *ghaybat*. This term has a peculiar meaning for Shi'is, suggesting not merely that God has ordained the concealment but that in doing so he has prolonged the life of the *imam* indefinitely by miraculous means.

What happened to Muhammad al-Mahdi subsequently is wreathed in mystery and it may be that he experienced a similar fate to that of his forebears. It is said, however, that he disappeared down a well in order to escape the fate that had befallen his father and grandfather and that his public duties were taken over by deputies, known as *bab* or *na'ib* before whom he may have appeared from time to time. These men included, in succession, 'Uthman al Amir, Abu Jafar Muhammad ibn 'Uthman, Abu'l Qasim Husayn ibn Ruh an Nawbakhti and Abu'l Husayn Ali ibn Muhammad as Samarri. The *babs* appointed agents or *wikala*, sometimes taking the job themselves, who would act as intermediaries between the *imam* and his followers.

The period during which the twelfth *imam* was allegedly in contact with the *babs* is known as the Lesser Occultation, the *ghaybat-i sughra*. It lasted for about 70 years and ended in 941 CE with the death of the fourth bab who, on his deathbed, is said to have produced a letter from Muhammad al-Mahdi giving instructions that no more deputies were to be appointed and that any tangible representation of the imamate was to cease. A tradition developed that the Hidden Imam would return as the *mahdi* either immediately before *qiyama*, the Day of Judgement, or at some other time in the future. The intervening period would continue for as long as Allah chooses and it became known as the Greater Occultation or *ghaybat-i kubra*. Shi'is tend to use the analogy that the Hidden Imam is like the sun behind clouds. He is hidden but still possesses the power to warm the spirits of the faithful. Shi'is believe that it is possible to send messages to the Hidden Imam and receive guidance by leaving notes at his various shrines.

Shi'a Muslims thus believe that, in an event known as *raj'a*, the *mahdi* will lead his people in a restoration of their status akin to the Second Coming of the Christian messiah that promised not only to restore the greatness of the Jewish nation but also to be the salvation of all humankind from the consequences of its own weakness. The *mahdi* is, in fact, often identified with Jesus Christ and it is imagined that he will appear somewhere in Syria or Palestine. He will sweep away the influence of the Anti-Christ, justice and peace will be re-established all over the world and Islam will triumph.

For a follower of mainstream Sunna, the interpretation of *mahdi* is somewhat looser. Sunnis discount the tradition of the twelfth *imam*, pointing out that, were he genuinely in hiding, he would by now have been alive for over 12 centuries, which is rather a long time in terms of human life-span. It is also argued that, since Allah is omnipotent, he has no need to keep a man alive for tens of centuries since he can create a new leader at will when the time is appropriate. Critics also make the observation that, by nature, an *imam* is there to guide his people and that if he is in perennial hiding any purpose attached to his existence is negated. For Sunnis, *mahdi* refers to one who is divinely guided and the title has been accorded to, or rather adopted by, several historical personalities, strong and charismatic people who have wished to lead Muslims during difficult times of oppression and conflict when restoration or bolstering of the faith was needed.

Many of the would-be *mahdis* emerged, not surprisingly, from the mystical Sufi movement (see p. 124), spurred by the romantic idea that they could lead the world revolution to peace and good order that Islam predicts will take place before the end of time. At the turn of the sixteenth century in India a celebrated contender, 'Alid Muhammad of Jaunpur, claimed the title of *mahdi* and to this day there are those who believe that he was indeed the chosen one and that his resurrection will come about to presage the end of the world. Perhaps the best known of such remarkable men in recent centuries was Muhammad Ahmad ibn 'Abdullah (1844–85), who claimed not

Below: *An 1884 engraving of the British military encampment at Souakin in the Sudan during the Mahdi uprisings. In the foreground an Egyptian mother selling vegetables nurses her baby.*

only to be the *mahdi* but also a descendant of the Prophet Muhammad. Having emerged from a fundamentalist religious fraternity committed to restoration of Islamic discipline and purity as it had been in the time of the Prophet, he established and headed a religious state in the Sudan. It flourished during the period between 1882 and 1898, having first taken on and driven out the British and Egyptian forces under General Gordon who was defeated at Khartoum in 1885 after a 10-month siege. Ironically the holy war was fought by the *mahdi* against the Muslim government of Egypt, an Islamic kingdom, whose forces had invaded the Sudan in 1820. Egypt, however, had fallen under European influence and was dependent on European power to maintain its position. It was this dilution of the faith that primarily offended Muhammad Ahmad ibn 'Abdullah.

At times in the past these fanatical visionaries have also run into conflict with more mainstream leaders of Muslim communities. The Imam 'Abd al-Qadir whose resistance against French occupation of Algeria has been described, was challenged by a would-be *mahdi*, Muhammad ibn 'Abdullah, who preached that he was the long-awaited deliverer of Islam. Like other contenders for the title he had emerged from one of the mystical religious fraternities of Sufism, the Darqawa, a fringe group that had already been in active resistance against Ottoman colonialism. Not surprisingly 'Abd al-Qadir took exception to this challenge to his authority and attacked those tribal groups that had elected to support Muhammad ibn 'Abdullah, defeating them in about 1840.

ULEMA

Among the mainstream Sunni, the leaders of communities are generally members of the *ulema*, the body of religious and legal clerics or scholars. The word *ulema* simply means "learned men". They form a distinct social class in Islamic countries where Sunnis predominate and earn their recognition only after having studied extensively under established teachers. The *ulema* should not be thought of as priests in the Christian sense that people take up an evangelizing and pastoral vocation, but they occupy an important place in Muslim society nonetheless as the keepers and interpreters of *Shari'a*, the religious law of Islam. This covers a wide spectrum from the Five Pillars of Islam (see p. 104) through marriage and inheritance rulings, commercial legislation, criminal law, rules concerning purity and diet and relationships with non-Muslims. Historically, during the time of the Umayyad caliphate, the *ulema* were to be distinguished by the first wearing of the turban as a symbol of their rank.

Below: *A group of Muslim legal scholars, known locally as moulvees, discuss aspects of law in Delhi, India.*

Mujtahid and ayatollah

In Shi'a communities, the comparable body of scholars is that of the *mujtahids* and in Iran the most senior echelons of these intellectuals take the title of *ayatollah*, sometimes spelled *ayatullah*, and, ultimately, *imam* (though not in the Twelver sense). These men constitute the nearest approach to what in the West we might think of as clergy. The term *ayatollah* is a contraction of the Arabic *ayat Allah*, meaning "Miraculous sign from God". The title is, however, peculiar to Iran and is not used by Shi'is in other countries such as Iraq where the equivalent senior clerics are known as *marja al-taqlid*, literally, a "reference source to be emulated". The position of *marja al-taqlid* has been recognized since before the seventeenth century and the rulings of these senior legislators have become binding on other clerics lower down the order.

The title *ayatollah* was first coined in Iran during the nineteenth century but in recent times it has gained a dubious reputation outside of the Islamic sphere. The sensitivity has arisen not least because of the reputation in the West earned by the late Ayatollah Ruhollah Khomeini, who rose to prominence as the outstanding religious leader and founder of the Islamic Republic of Iran after the expulsion of the Shah, Muhammad Riza Pahlavi, but who also became associated with strong anti-Western sentiment and militarism.

Ayatollah Khomeini

Born on September 24, 1902 at Khomayn, a small town lying about 100 kilometres south-west of Tehran, Ruhollah al-Musavi al-Khomeini lost his father, Ayatollah al-Mustafa, to assassination when an infant and he was raised by his mother and an aunt. From his late teenage years onwards he studied religious sciences and spiritual philosophy at a school in the nearby town of Arak under the guidance of Shaikh 'Abd al-Karim Ha'iri, and it was there that he first came into contact with political activism.

The 1930s found him lecturing in religious philosophy and ethics in the city of Qum, where his classes attracted large numbers of students. By that stage of his life he had already gained acceptance as an authoritative writer and he gradually became identified as a critic of the regime of the Shah Riza who established the Pahlavi state, turning the Iranian monarchy into a totalitarian dictatorship essentially resistant to Islam as a cultural and political influence. Towards the end of the decade and after the death of his old mentor 'Abd al-Karim Ha'iri, Khomeini supported the nomination of Ayatollah Burujirdi as head of the Iranian religious body, anticipating that Burujirdi was the best placed cleric to provide opposition against Pahlavi rule. Khomeini was to be disappointed, however, since Burujirdi spent his period in office largely side-stepping any political controversy. After Burujirdi's death in 1962 Khomeini was one of the few individuals prepared to risk speaking out against the Pahlavi regime and he became accepted by an increasing number of Muslims as the voice of opposition.

Later in 1962 relations between the Shah and the clerical leaders in Iran deteriorated markedly after the Pahlavi government promoted new legislation abolishing the long-established requirement that candidates for election to local assemblies should be both male and of Muslim persuasion. This law was not particularly significant since the function of assembly representatives was largely formal and lacked any political muscle but it was seen by many as a gesture of goodwill towards the United States to ensure continuing financial and political support for the regime. It therefore provided a convenient catalyst with which to raise the temperature of dissent among a populace that already held little affection for the West. So, the Iranian religious institution mounted a strong protest, gained considerable backing at street level and the ruling was eventually repealed. The action was to mark the beginning of the end for the Pahlavi dynasty.

In 1963 there was further erosion of popular support for the Shah as he pursued a radical policy of Westernization. Much of the criticism emanated from Ayatollah Khomeini in Qum, where he was actively preaching dissent in his school, the Fayziya *madrasa*. He denounced the regime of the Shah as a tyranny bent on increasing links with Israel and with the United States. The response of government was swift and in March, troops took over the Fayziya school during a violent assault in which several students were killed. A month or so later Khomeini was arrested for subversive activities, protest demonstrations followed and the number of activist deaths in various Iranian cities rose sharply in consequence. Although the uprising was suppressed and Khomeini was released, he was perceived to be an ongoing threat to stability and in November 1964 he was arrested again and exiled first to Turkey and then to Najaf, a Shi'a stronghold in Iraq, where he lived for the next 13 years and was to become the rallying point for the Islamic revolution in Iran in 1978. From time to time Khomeini made pronouncements against the Shah's government and, in effect, stood for a Muslim administration in exile.

Above: *Ayatollah Ruhollah Khomeini prays with some of his adherents in the garden of his villa at Pontchartrain, near Paris, during his exile from Iran in 1982.*

Khomeini's conduct did not go unnoticed in Iran and in September 1978, the Baathist government of Iraq was persuaded to expel him as a subversive plotting the overthrow of a neighbouring country's legitimate government. No Muslim state was willing to accept him as a refugee unless he was prepared to agree to curb his political activities and so, in October, he moved to a new exile in Europe, taking a house in a small village near Paris. There he found the freedom he desired to carry on his crusade against the regime of the shah and with it his reputation grew. Ironically he found that he had better facilities to disseminate his message to the Iranian people from France than from Iraq. Pronouncements were recorded onto cassette tapes and distributed through an underground network. In January 1979, the Shah of Iran abdicated and a month later the Iranian Bakhtiar government that

Right: *A young boy perched on his father's shoulders holds up a portrait of Ayatollah Khomeini during protests in Teheran in December 1978 demanding the end of the Shah's rule in Iran*

had supported the monarchy collapsed. Ayatollah Khomeini was free to return to his home country and in February was elected to lead the first government of the Islamic Republic of Iran, becoming the Imam Khomeini. His predictably radical policy was to remove all Western influence from Iran, to found a new Shi'a religious state and, in so doing, to instigate a cultural revolution. Many people consider that he went too far in his zeal and that, in particular, he was responsible for extending the Gulf War against Iraq, which ultimately cost tens of thousands of lives on both sides. Khomeini died in 1989 after a long battle with cancer.

Originally the *ayatollahs* were those who had reached the penultimate plane of the Shi'a religious hierarchy, one step below that of *imam*, but towards the end of the Iranian monarchy, some of them, including Khomeini, took on the responsibility for interpreting and passing judgement in matters of faith and practice. Those who came across as being particularly charismatic earned the recognition and acclaim of the population and were feted in a manner akin to that of celebrities. Today the title can be taken by virtually any jurist and, in consequence, the most senior ranks earn the distinction of being *al-Uzma* or "supreme".

MULLAH

Among the lower ranks of men schooled in religious affairs are the *mullahs*. In Iran, Turkey and India ordinary teachers in Muslim schools and men who expound on sacred law earn this title as a mark of respect. In Turkey a *mullah* is also a provincial magistrate. In India among Shi'a Muslims the term can refer specifically to the spiritual leader or dai during the present time of the Hidden Imam. But a *mullah* may also be a more fanatical individual, a preacher of aggressive response to the infidel. Men who have joined this category in recent times include Mullah Muhammad Omar, the extremist Taliban leader in Afghanistan who was proclaimed *Amir al-Mu'mineen* (Commander of the Faithful) by subscribers to his fundamentalist interpretation of Islam. It would be wrong, however, to assume that all prominent Muslim clerics are of the same belligerent persuasion. Recently one of Kabul's foremost clerics Mullah Abdul Raouf, who had been banned by the Taliban regime from preaching in his own Kwaj Ali Mofeq Herawee mosque, proclaimed that Mullah Muhammad Omar was "A defender of killers, not the defender of the faithful" and urged that Omar should be tried by an international tribunal. The Qur'an, he pointed out, does not encourage capital punishment but equally provides for just retribution under certain circumstances.

WALI

Beneath such levels of scholarship as *ayatollah* and *mullah* is the *wali*, who is very much a "grass-roots" inspiration to ordinary people, less distant in body and spirit than more senior figures in the hierarchy. He is, or was, a local holy man considered to possess good saintly attributes and therefore to be "nearer to Allah". In this favoured position he has earned a reputation for his prophetic utterances and his ability to perform miracles of healing. The *wali* is also believed to act as intercessor acting for the benefit of both the living and the dead.

KHALIFA

The title *khalifa* or, in its Anglicized form "caliph" also needs a proper introduction. The word is an abbreviation of the term *khalifatu rasulil-lah*, which can be interpreted as "Successor to the Messenger of Allah". The first man to assume the accolade *khalifa* after the death of Muhammad was Abu Bakr. He coined the term and the *khalifa* became the recognized head of the Muslim community during the dynasties of the Umayyads and the Abassids, prior to the expansion of the Mongol Empire that took over most of the Muslim-controlled lands in the Middle Ages. Sunni Muslims regard the first four of these caliphs to have enjoyed legitimate claim to the title, the "four rightly guided caliphs". Shi'is reject the legitimacy of the first three, Abu Bakr, 'Umar and 'Uthman and only accept that of the fourth incumbent, 'Ali, claiming that it was he and his descendants who had been ordained as leaders by Muhammad.

Following page: Early 17th-century portrait of an aged mullah, by Farrukh Beg. Mughal.

THE ISLAMIC LAW – SHARI'A

Shari'a, a word that means "the clear path", is the sacred law of Islam and in Muslim society it is considered to be of greater importance even than theology. Every decision, every judgement made by men of the *ulema*, the body of learned men, in effect descends from this religious or canonical legislature and adherence to it is the duty of each male Muslim who is of sound mind and who is mature enough to be responsible for his own actions. Usually the determining age for compliance with Shari'a is at about 15 or at puberty. Today it represents the common ideal of Islamic society, yet its roots are buried in a pre-Islamic tribal organization. This aspect is particularly important because Arab society, since time immemorial, had been (and remains) immensely conservative. In life one follows the customs that one's father and grandfather followed. One maintains precedent or *sunna*. If there was an outstanding obstacle to the smooth development of Islam it was, ironically, this passion for tradition. Change was viewed with considerable suspicion. Nonetheless it was clear to Muhammad that a time had come for change and once it did, the *"sunna* of the Prophet" became sufficiently important to be introduced as a central plank of Islamic law.

In early pre-Islamic society there had been no organized judicial system and disputes were settled in blood or by arbitration. In time, predictably, mediation was preferred to violence and rules of mediation were needed. So, the arbitrator also became the lawmaker and specialist who expounded the finer points of the law. When Islam arose in the seventh century, the Prophet Muhammad was called upon to settle disputes among his followers and so he effectively became the first person to adapt the old lawgiver's role to meet the needs of the new Muslim society. In this respect his intention seems not to have been to change existing Arab legislature but to provide a set of ground rules that would allow Muslims to fulfil their obligation to God and to their fellow human beings. The clearest example of moral legislation introduced by

Below: Muslim women members of the ulema, scholars of Islamic law, attending a lecture at the Al-Azhar University, Cairo in 1994.

Muhammad is that directed towards the welfare of family where, in pre-Islamic times, women, children and orphans were often treated very badly and sexual laxity was rife. In tribal society before the coming of Islam unwanted newborn girls were often buried alive and clearly Muhammad found such behaviour repugnant and in urgent need of amendment.

> *You shall not kill your children for fear of want.*
> *We shall provide for them and for you.*
> *To kill them is a great sin.*   (*Al-Isra:* 17. 31)

It is important for a Westerner to understand that the emphasis in the *Shari'a* is not first and foremost one of penalties but of morality. Sanctions are undoubtedly served on those who break its moral code and at times the punishments seem particularly harsh when one reads of floggings, of hands being cut off for theft and of public executions. But very often the penalties for breach of *Shari'a* were introduced much later in Islamic history and sometimes they resulted from a fairly loose interpretation of what the *Shari'a* and *hadith* had to say on a subject. In certain instances the law stands in clear contradiction to the doctrine contained in the Qur'an. An illustration lies in the penalty for the crime of adultery where the Qur'an is quite specific.

> *The adulterer and the adulteress shall each be given a hundred lashes.*
>   (*Al-Nur:* 24. 2)

Death by stoning for sexual indiscretion was introduced by the Medinan caliphs who claimed that they were able to interpret a verse of the Qur'an as justification for such a sentence. Some scholars now claim this verse to be spurious and there is wider indication that aspects of *hadith* were introduced retrospectively in order to justify a particular form of sentence.

Muhammad did not write the *Shari'a* as it is known today but he undoubtedly launched it in such a way that it could be further developed and expanded out of the old Arab arbitration procedure. This happened gradually during the early decades of Islam and as Muslim society came of age. The intellectuals who followed in Muhammad's wake as arbitrators of *Shari'a* became known as the *ulema* and they were recognized as the scholarly body of opinion in Islamic society.

Like the Jewish Ten Commandments, *Shari'a* is considered to be of divine origin, not man-made and it can be thought of as a complete system of responsibilities and obligations – ritual, ethical and legal. In Sunni tradition, as we have discovered, it is based on the holy writings of the Qur'an but takes into account the sayings of the Prophet Muhammad and certain rules prescribed by the early leaders of the Sunni sect. Thus it includes the Five Pillars of Islam – profession of the faith (*shahada*), worship (*salah*), charitable donation (*zakat*), pilgrimage (*hajj*) and fasting during Ramadan (*saum*). Shi'is also accept the Qur'an as the basis of *Shari'a* but add the

Opposite: Women enveloped in burqas walking past a mosque in Mazar-i-Sharif, Afghanistan, during the rule of the Taliban regime.

traditions of 'Ali and his descendants. In both communities a consensus of learned opinion about the interpretation is also deemed necessary.

When an *imam* or an *ayatollah* renders a judgement or a ruling it is invariably based on his interpretation of *Shari'a* but in the general sense *Shari'a* law also governs the way Muslims demonstrate their obedience to Islam whether in their individual or social life. In this way *Shari'a* contrasts with the inner, more private faith, which is referred to as *iman*. In Ottoman times *Shari'a* was distinguished from purely secular law known as *kanun*, but today, in principle at least, it represents the totality of the law in Islamic countries. However, it faces the same challenges as other examples of religious legislation that were laid down many centuries ago under wholly different social conditions.

Most Muslim countries have recognized that certain aspects of *Shari'a* are no longer strictly relevant in a modern society, particularly one that lives with global communications and large-scale international movement and is obliged to coexist alongside Western codes and values. Even in matters such as enforced marriage, the strict adherence to *Shari'a* is beginning to wane, as too are some of the more savage indictments, such as cutting off a man's hand for stealing. One of the most notorious punishments, in Western eyes, has been that of stoning for adultery. There are suggestions that such punishments were carried out from time to time by the Taliban in Afghanistan. By contrast in Iran, for instance, this penalty has not been carried out for many years and, were such a sentence to be passed today, it would first require three independent witnesses to the act, no easy matter in the circumstance of adultery.

It is, however, the conservatism of the Arab mentality, the resistance to any tendency for change, that has contributed to the violent behaviour of some fundamentalists who believe that any dilution of their religious tradition runs in direct conflict with the true spirit of the faith. Their desire is to return to a "golden age" of Islam, a time when Muslim civilization was at its zenith and when, as they see it, Western decadence did not intrude. Waves of popular fervour in such countries as Afghanistan, Iran, Pakistan and Sudan have raised the temperature with catch-phrases such as, "Islam is the Solution", but these countries also experience considerable internal differences of opinion about how far a return to Muslim fundamentalism should progress. Today's most talked of illustration is the turmoil engendered in Afghanistan under the recent Taliban regime, where any form of entertainment was effectively banned and where the rights of women were suppressed, but other countries have seen their share of Islamic fundamentalism in recent years. In Algeria, for example, Kamereddine Kherbane founded the Islamic Salvation Front in 1989 in direct opposition to the military establishment that has maintained power since independence from France was gained in 1962. The growth of his ISF party triggered considerable unrest and this has resulted in the imprisonment of activists and cancelling of parliamentary elections by the government in order to thwart the establishment of a fundamentalist Islamic state.

FATWA

Within Islamic law undoubtedly the most notorious term to a Western mind is *fatwa*. Few can be unaware of the *fatwa* once issued by Ayatollah Khomeini on the writer Salman Rushdie for what was viewed as blasphemy against the Prophet contained in his book *The Satanic Verses*, yet the meaning of the word *fatwa* may not be fully understood and is often given more lurid colours than it deserves in the Western press. Many Westerners probably view it as an edict or sentence, often of violent nature, passed by an Islamic cleric. It is not, however, purely a punishment in the sense of a judge handing down a sentence, although it may take this form under certain circumstances. In practice *fatwa* simply describes the legal interpretation of some or other aspect of *Shari'a*. Problems arise, as in any political or religious system, when an arbiter of the law adopts a despotic or unreasonable position in order to exploit the system. Under these circumstances *fatwa* can mutate into something akin to violent retribution or vendetta.

JIHAD

Scarcely less publicized is *jihad*, a term that has also been widely misunderstood and misused. Ask most Westerners what they understand by *jihad* and they will tell you it means a "holy war". Yet the expression "holy war" was coined not by Muslims but Christians during the crusades. To a Muslim, *jihad* translates rather differently – it means "striving". Very often *jihad* is a struggle that the follower of Islam conducts within himself or herself but since Islam is seen to encompass all of humanity the striving can also extend to the local community or even the world at large. It is reflected in the Qur'anic ideal that Muslims must pursue good and resist evil at whatever level of society.

The means whereby pursuit of good at the expense of evil is achieved can of course vary. It may be achieved through political diplomacy or by legal means but if these fail Islam permits the use of force, much as Western-style democracies may take up arms as a last resort. The Qur'an instructs Muslims unequivocally:

> *Make peace between them [the protagonists], but if one persists in aggression against the other, fight the aggressors until they revert to God's commandment.* (Al-Hujurat: 49. 9)

What may appear just and ethically right to one party in such a conflict is invariably outrageous and indefensible to the other. Problems can arise when Western values and opinions do not reflect the Islamic ideal that has brought about a military-style *jihad*. Often the majority of Muslim opinion does not support extremist activity either. Such was clearly the case in the September 11, 2001, assault on the World Trade Centre in New York when not only the non-Islamic world but also most Muslims shared repugnance over what had been perpetrated by the fanatical few in the name of *jihad*.

ISLAM TODAY & TOMORROW

ALTHOUGH STATISTICS ARE HARD TO COME BY, IT IS BELIEVED THAT there are between 600 and 1,000 million Muslims scattered through 48 countries of the globe. If this figure is anywhere near accurate then the number of Islamic faithful in the world today more or less equals the number of Roman Catholics. As in the case of Christianity, in some countries conversion to Islam is on the increase, in others Islam is static and in some it is on the wane.

Most of the Islamic world is now independent, in the sense that few of its nation states are under colonial rule or domination. Among the notable exceptions are Palestine that still struggles to escape partition with Israel and the Muslim states in the southern part of the old Soviet Union. It was calculated in the 1970s that some 17 million Muslims

lived in the European Soviet territories where they experienced considerable repression and although those numbers have now increased they still experience problems. Today, in Azerbaijan, for example, more than 93 per cent of the population are practising Muslims.

Elsewhere, foreign dominance by and large came to an end over a period of years after the Second World War, when the imperial possessions of the British, Dutch and French were slowly given away. Most of the transitions to Islamic sovereignty were easy and amicable. Only in a few cases was the struggle to gain independence drawn out and bloody. Probably the most notable of these local areas of conflict was France's tenacious hold over Algeria that continued until the 1990s. Generally, colonial dominance had left Islam with a legacy of Western values, Western culture and Western exploitation, particularly in respect of one commodity in the Middle Eastern Muslim countries, oil. It was not entirely a one-sided process. During the nineteenth century and later Muslim leaders had also cast a covetous eye on the material benefits enjoyed by the European colonial powers and wanted their slice of the cake. They saw the advantage of railways, electricity, plumbing, telephone services and, above all, of obtaining some of the military hardware on display. Since 1945, as independence has spread, a vast amount of armaments has been sold to emergent Islamic nations, which, in the Middle East, have traded oil for guns. From being a commodity exploited by the West, oil has become the most powerful political bargaining chip of the nations from whose soil it gushes.

Islamic states extend from Europe to Africa and as far eastwards as Indonesia, though they are still mainly concentrated in the Middle East among the Arab peoples. The populations of some of these countries are growing at a tremendous rate. In Iran, for

Above: *A Shi'a Muslim father and daughter pose for the camera in June 2000 at Persepolis, Iran.*

Previous page: *A symbol of modernity and western influence in Islam. A girl drinks soda through a straw in the Muslim quarter of Jerusalem, Israel.*

example, the population in 1996 was calculated to be not less than 66 million, of whom 95 per cent are Shi'a Muslims. The population of Iran is currently growing at nearly 2.5 per cent annually. In other parts of the world minority Muslim communities are also expanding dramatically, nowhere more so than in the industrialized centres of Europe. These have seen, and continue to experience, massive influxes of Muslim workers and white-collar professionals from the poorer regions of the Balkans, North Africa, Pakistan and Indonesia.

Surprisingly, perhaps, given the nature of the rhetoric emanating from some Islamic leaders, about five million Muslims live in the United States, the land of the "Great

Satan" and there are no less than 1,000 mosques scattered throughout North America. The influx began during the colonial period when African slaves brought the religion to the continent, although many of these forced immigrants found it more expedient for their welfare under the eyes of plantation owners to convert to Christianity. Many more arrived during the nineteenth century as part of the rush of immigrant workers on ships from Eastern Europe and the Arab countries, tired of a punishing existence under colonial rule, lured by the promise of freedom, money and a better standard living. In the United States some ten national associations are now devoted exclusively to Muslim affairs and the country plays host to 18 Muslim embassies.

Nonetheless all is not well and recent events have highlighted the malaise. Since the Second World War many European countries have seen an influx of Muslim workers who arrived on a temporary basis but then gradually built permanent communities in the major cities. In some places these have descended into little better than ghettos. The immigrant communities tend to be younger than native populations, to bring with them a religious culture that they prefer to that of their hosts and to have larger families. This can quickly cause resentment when unemployment is already running at a high level among native workers. When outspoken fundamentalists exist among these communities and are willing to stir up cultural unrest, they very often find themselves at odds with the norms of behaviour in the host country and violence can speedily ensue.

There is much to criticize in the tangled story of faith. It is true to say, sadly, that religious conflict in today's world is as much alive and kicking as it ever was. It is only the machinery and place of strife that ever changes and more or less all religions, with the possible exception of Buddhism, must own up to militant histories.

A problem in gaining any balanced view of Islam in the year 2002, therefore, is that dramatic events that capture newspaper and TV headlines and that focus on

Below: *New York Muslim men pray at a mosque on East 96th Street, on the day after the attack on the World Trade Center in New York.*

religious conflict have tended to distract from and even disguise the broader picture. One has to venture no further than the internet, a cyber realm still largely dominated by American contribution and commentary, to discover that by entering "modern Islam" as search words, one is led to a plethora of web pages devoted almost exclusively to the perceived Muslim "threat". This danger comes in the form of the Taliban regime, Osama bin Laden, the issue of Palestine, Saddam Hussein, the absence of democracy in the Islamic world and so on. Most articles have religious overtones suggesting "My God is better than your God". It would be wrong to suggest that the rhetoric is all one-sided, but that emanating from the Muslim side tends to be broadcast through other vehicles within the Islamic community.

It is undoubtedly true that the Islamic and non-Islamic worlds are at loggerheads over a number of key issues. To offer one obvious example, the Western world, by and large, views Osama bin Laden as a terrorist to be eliminated at all cost. Yet in other parts of the globe the same man is a hero. He is revered by many people in the Middle East and in the Philippines he is accorded celebrity status akin to that of a pop star. A worrying polarization has come about and a recent disclosure by Dr George Carey, Archbishop of Canterbury, revealed the extent of concern in some quarters over the potential for eruption into wider conflict that these differences in view contain. He and the foremost Shi'a *imam*, Dr Muhammad Sayid Tantawy, the Head of the Al-Azhar School in Cairo, have joined forces in order to establish better channels of communication between Christian and Muslim communities.

A few years ago, in December 1997, George Carey was invited to the International Islamic University in Islamabad, Pakistan, where he gave a lecture on the Duty of Religion within the Human Family. He made an important observation that, because both Islam and Christianity claim to be universal religions, there exists a potential for strife between them, particularly so when the world is shrinking in terms of communication and ease of travel. He went on to say that we all have a duty to look carefully at the balance between making disciples on the one hand, and maintaining respect for alternative faiths on the other. Dr Carey argued that claims made about faith are essentially invitations to others of different religious persuasion to consider that our experience and what it has meant to us may also be something that can transform them.

It is difficult at the dawn of the twenty-first century to see that Dr Carey's ideal is working particularly well and he admits that the violence before us, whether in Birmingham, Cairo or Jerusalem, is often linked to religious fervour which springs from the more militant and passionate members of different faith communities. He was forced to concede that the same religions which possess the potential to create bonds between communities have all too often divided and alienated people from one another. Secular concerns can feed the non-secular where different cultures fear that each is threatening the welfare of the other. Issues of poverty and despair, to take just two examples, can become intertwined with issues of faith and can result in aggression. Nowhere is this perhaps more true than in the ongoing Palestinian situation.

In recognition of the problems from the Muslim viewpoint, the Rector of the International Islamic University, Dr Maraj Khalid, is quoted as saying, during a lecture at the Al-Ahzar University, that the Western mind needs to rid itself of deep-rooted biases about Islam and the Muslims, while Muslims need equally to reorientate themselves and examine critically their own assumptions about the West. That these biases exist is clear. An independent Catholic discussion forum on the web informs us that "Islam is one hundred percent heresy despite its borrowing of the Judao-Christian Traditions. The denial of Christ as God Incarnate is enough to know that Islam is the greatest threat to mankind's salvation in Christ." Similar vehemence is just as easy to discover among a limited number of Islamic web sites.

One of the root causes of friction is that the two systems of political ideology are, in some respects, seen to be incompatible. The West prides itself on being a defender of democracy while, in many Western eyes, Muslim countries amount to totalitarian regimes where recognized democratic rules either do not apply or are not adequately maintained. If everyone is subject to the rules and regulations laid down by Allah then how can people claim to live in a democracy? This a rather simplistic question because, in Saudi Arabia for example, the laws of society in practice rest in the hands not of Allah but of the ruling royal house and its political administrators. Likewise in Afghanistan, it was not God but the Taliban who dictated the harsh way of life. If there is an underlying problem it lies in the despotism of those who sometimes govern Muslim countries in the name of Islam and even in the name of democracy. Islamic countries are, of course, not alone in the modern world in fostering despotic

Below: *Visions of the future. A modernistic mosque finds building space between the skyscrapers of Abu Dhabi in the United Arab Emirates.*

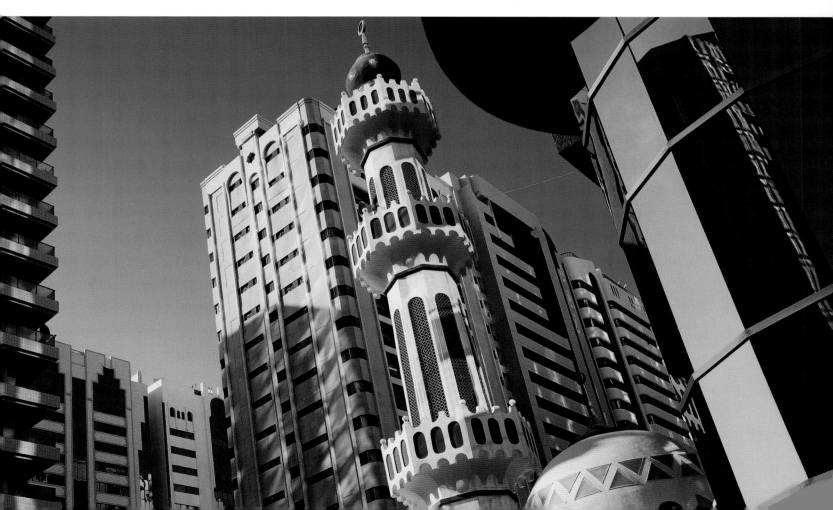

regimes but there is also a twist in the tale. There is an argument, not without substance, that Western policy-makers are actually reluctant to see democracy replace autocracy, particularly in the Middle East where maintaining the status quo is paramount in the eyes of the West because of reliance on oil. Putting it crudely, replacement of the Saudi royal family or the other emirates of the Gulf with popularly elected governments might sound a fine argument in the ears of human rights activists, but what would it bring in their stead? Quite possibly the kind of chaos seen in Afghanistan recently: a radical Islamic government propelled into power on a wave of religious fervour, not only breaking away from accepted norms of international diplomacy but perhaps diametrically opposed to parting with its oil wealth for the benefit of capitalists.

Above: *A sign in a Malaysian mosque reminds people to remove their shoes and be quiet.*

The view from the other side of the ideological divide can be equally off the mark. Many Muslims see modern democracy as something essentially decadent and alien to a way of life in which one is answerable to God and in which old traditions are best. Yet liberalized democracy and a secular way of life do not necessarily have to be bedfellows. The truth is that little in Islam conflicts with principles of democracy and, by similar token, few aspects of Western-style politics are at odds with a life devoted to the laws of God.

Whatever people's religious persuasion may be, one change that has taken place in the last 30 years lies in the focus of world attention on armed aggression, an issue never far from hearts and minds. In the late 1990s there was a prominent theory in circulation that all civilizations are founded in conflict. Evidence was offered that the earliest cities known to archaeology are characterized by a predominance of artwork depicting scenes of warfare and by deposits of weapons. Man, in other words, needs someone to fight with in order to be happy. This theory about the origins of civilization has now been largely disproved but it remains true that virtually all civilized societies throughout history have found the excuse to be uncivilized towards one another and more often than not the banner of ideology, whether parading as religion or some other principle, has flown in the vanguard of battle.

From the end of the Second World War, and with the demise of the old empire blocs, the eyes of the world were focused on a potential clash of titans in the shape of the United States and the Soviet Union. Everything else paled into insignificance beside the thought of nuclear annihilation at the hands of the superpowers. But that particular alarm has receded and it seems to be a quirk of human nature that something must take its place, to provide us with potential dangers against which we must defend by force of arms if necessary. The Western world has discovered a new source of worry in Islamic fundamentalism and the terror tactics with which it is frequently accompanied. It would be wrong, however, to imagine this worry amounting to a threat of Muslim countries taking up arms against non-Muslim countries or vice versa, as some of the more lurid newspaper analyses have suggested recently: the rise of Islam against the West. The reality is that while the global threat of terrorism is now very real and much of it is rooted in Muslim extremism, Islam is thoroughly diverse in its politics and behaviour. There can be no greater contrasts than between the socialist radicalism of Libya and the conservatism of the regimes in Saudi Arabia and Pakistan, or between the populist despotism seen in Iraq and the cleric-dominated theocracy of Iran. Within this spectrum, at national level, far more Islamic states are moderate and willing to live in a world of peace and social justice, than are radical, militant and fundamentalist in their ideals. Likewise, the majority of Muslim organizations turn to the ballot box and dialogue, not terrorism and the suicide bomb.

Of one thing we can be certain. From the 1970s onwards Islamic fervour, freed from colonial restrictions, was resurgent throughout the world. There is no clear explanation of why this revival happened, although the defeat of the Arab nations by Israel in 1967 may have provided one of several catalysts. Another was perhaps the civil war in Pakistan that took place a few years later, leading to the creation of Bangladesh. Here, on the one hand, was a group of Arab Muslim states failing to acquit themselves effectively, and on the other a Muslim country was openly at war with itself, revealing that the bond supposedly keeping the faithful under the one green banner of Islam was not as strong as might have been imagined. Islamic leaders with an eye on the past will also have been painfully aware that both poor military leadership and infighting had been the cause of downfall in more than one Muslim Empire throughout 1,500 years of history. These painful situations and others revealed that secular nationalism among Muslims who were ethnically and culturally diverse was not a particularly effective binding agent nor had it led to prosperity or military success. People often toiled under despotic regimes supported by the West, of which the Pahlavi dynasty in Iran is a prime example, and they were seeking a new form of identity. They found it, just as Muhammad had in the sixth century, in a fresh blossoming of religious ideals and a revitalized spiritual focus to their lives.

Left: *A copy of the Qur'an at Sultanahmet.*

Opposite: *Pilgrims in tens of thousands gather at the Great Mosque in Mecca, Saudi Arabia during the hajj. In the middle distance the Ka'aba stands shrouded in its dark cloth covering.*

If it is possible to find a third trigger for Islamic resurgence, it is perhaps in the remarkable chain of events which saw the popular overthrow of the Shah in Iran and his replacement by a charismatic cleric who founded the first genuinely Islamic republic of modern times. It is interesting that many of the leaders of former nationalist movements switched ideologies and became the founders of new Islamic movements that were popular because they were seen to be in the pockets neither of capitalists nor communists. Capitalism brought with it materialistic values that had already been seen to erode religious ideals in Muslim countries where it had been allowed to gain a foothold; communism would have denied these ideals altogether. Paradoxically, many of today's Islamic elite, doctors, lawyers, high-ranking military officers, have benefited from education either in the West or in Western-style schools. Yet they have returned to their homelands to champion Muslim causes and Islamic systems of government.

From the 1960s, from a combination of setbacks and new leaderships, the desire emerged for unity and for religious and cultural identity among Muslim nations. The smell of reform was in the air against the Western influences that had been gathering and infiltrating Islamic society. It was also realized that internecine squabbling would achieve nothing while cooperation provided a way forward. In 1962 the Muslim World League was established, with its headquarters sited symbolically in Mecca. In 1969 Muslim leaders from 57 states sat down together for the first time under the umbrella of the Organization of the Islamic Conference. The intention was, and still is, to pool resources and speak with one voice to safeguard mutual interests as well as the well-being of Muslims everywhere in the world.

Other organizations emerged of a more non-secular nature, most of them peaceful in outlook and primarily concerned to raise awareness about the old traditional Islamic values inherent in the Shari'a. Only a few have turned to extreme forms of fundamentalism and violence in their desire to eliminate Western style norms of living. Dominating the list in the eyes of the West is, of course, Al Quaeda, but such violent exceptions should not be taken as representative of Islam. The Muslim world is primarily concerned to re-establish its rightful identity, to provide its people with better standards of living and learning, to adopt Western ideas in science and technology where these are seen to be constructive, to offer the benefits of its own science and learning to the West and to live in peace with its neighbours.

As to whether the drive for traditional values based on religious law will make any real progress in the twenty-first century, it is doubtful. In most countries where the Muslim population is in a minority, followers of Islam are governed by national secular law that takes precedence over any desire to live strictly by Shari'a. Even in nation states such as Turkey where Muslims form a majority, secular law often holds sway over any other. In would-be fundamentalist states like Iran and Afghanistan, extreme theocratic rule has been either watered down fairly quickly or thrown out altogether. It may be, ultimately, when the fires of passion and the desire for identity have died down that Muslims will become increasingly like Christians in the sense that their religion becomes less of a national struggle, more of personal and private quest to find God.

INDEX

PICTURE CREDITS

The publishers would like to thank the following sources for their kind permission to reproduce the pictures in this book:

Ancient Art & Architecture Collection: 15, 24, 26, 34, 41, 66, 73, 76, 78, 82, 83, 86, 108, 117, 124, 128, 129, 134tl, 137tr, 150, 151tr, 157tr, 158, 174; **AKG London**: 3, 4, 13, 38, 90, 92, 93, 136; /Hedda Eid: 134br; /Jean-Louis Nou: 72; **Art Archive**: 163; /British Library, London: 33, 154; /Dagli Orti: 25, 27, 127, 144; /National Library, Cairo/Dagli Orti: 39; /Turkish & Islamic Art Museum, Istanbul /Dagli Orti: 9, 22, 23, 43, 114, 122; /Turkish & Islamic Art Museum, Istanbul/Harper Collins: 18, 21, 36, 42, 44, 50, 52, 56, 125; /Topkapi Museum, Istanbul/Dagli Orti: 29, 54, 80, 81, 148, 152, 159; /Topkapi Museum, Istanbul/Harper Collins: 45, 48, 49, 51; /Galleria degli Uffizi, Florence/Dagli Orti: 11; /Victoria & Albert Museum, London/Eileen Tweedy: 153; **Bodleian Library, University of Oxford**: MS. Pococke 375 folio 3v-4r: 20; **Bridgeman Art Library**: Bibliotheque Nationale, Paris: 12, 28; /Bibliotheque Nationale, Tunis/Bridgeman Giraudon/Lauros: 88; /British Library, London: 75; /Chester Beatty Library, Dublin: 126; /Hamburg Kunsthalle, Hamburg: 106-107, 109; /Iman Zahdah Chah Zaid Mosque, Isfahan/Index: 59, 64, 118; /Institute of Oriental Studies, St. Petersburg: 84, 87; /Private Collection/The Stapleton Collection: 104; /Seattle Art Museum, Seattle: 46, 47; /Victoria & Albert Museum, London: 105; **Corbis**: 58, 131, 139, 168; /Paul Almasy: 96, 100; /Archivo Iconografico: 55, 77, 156; /Dave Bartruff: 182; /Bettmann: 151b, 171, 172; /Burstein Collection: 164; /Gérard Degeorge: 1, 10, 178; /Sergio Dorantes: 140; /Owen Franken: 161; /Michael Freeman: 101; /Annie Griffiths Belt: 69, 180; /Lindsay Hebberd: 16; /Jon Hicks: 185; /Historical Picture Archive: 169; /Angelo Hornak: 145bl; /Hulton Archive: 94, 98; /Earl & NazimaKowall: 157bl; /David Lees: 2, 120-121; /Charles& Josette Lenars: 63, 65, 147; /Samer Mohdad: 175; /Richard T. Nowitz: 133, 145tr; /Bernd Obermann: 183; /Charles O'Rear: 102; /Christine Osborne: 119, 137bl; /Steve Raymer: 112, 186; /David Rubinger: 95; /Joseph Sohm/ChromoSohm: 141; /Jon Spaull: 177; /Ted Spiegel: 71; /Chase Swift: 70; /Arthur Thévenart: 110, 111; /Nik Wheeler: 113, 135, 166; /WildCountry: 142; /Roger Wood: 130, 138; /Adam Woolfitt: 8; /Michael S. Yamashita: 146, 160, 162; **Getty Images**: Nabeel Turner: 189; /Stefano Scata: 187; **Mary Evans Picture Library**: 60; **Travel Ink**: Stephen Coyne: 30; **Werner Forman Archive**: Mrs Bashir Mohamed Collection: 91; /Victoria & Albert Museum, London: 6.

Every effort has been made to acknowledge correctly and contact the source and/or copyright holder of each picture, and Carlton Books Limited apologises for any unintentional errors or omissions which will be corrected in future editions of this book.